THE BOOK I NEEDED

AWAKEN, ALIGN & EMBODY

A guide to breaking free and living with soulful clarity.

PREFACE

I remember sitting on the edge of my bed one night, scrolling endlessly through my phone, my chest heavy but my face smiling for everyone else. I was exhausted by pretending, pretending to be fine at work, pretending to be grateful in family gatherings, pretending to love myself when I barely recognized the woman in the mirror.

That night, I realized I wasn't just tired. I was absent from my own life.

This absence is what this book speaks to. It is about the silent ways we abandon ourselves in relationships, in roles, in expectations, and the powerful ways we can return.

This book is not meant to be consumed like advice but lived like a conversation. It asks you not only to think differently but to breathe differently, to pause, to listen to the body you have long ignored.

The pages ahead are both a mirror and an invitation. A mirror to help you recognize the masks and patterns that were never yours to carry. An invitation to step into alignment, to live not from fear but from soul.

If you have ever felt the quiet ache of disconnection, the

weight of roles you didn't choose, or the longing to feel whole again, this book is for you.

ACKNOWLEDGMENTS

This book would not have been possible without the invisible and visible threads that supported me during my own unravelling.

To those who unknowingly mirrored my wounds, and to those who held space for my healing, thank you. You were all integral to this transformation.

To my teachers, both earthly and energetic, who provided me with the tools of self-inquiry, truth, and embodiment, I bow to your presence on my path.

To my family and lineage, thank you for the lessons, the patterns, and the deep karmic work that shaped this exploration.

To the people I have loved, lost, confronted, resisted, and grown alongside, your presence has left an imprint on these pages more than you will ever know.

To my closest circle, who believed in the power of this message before it was ever written, thank you for your energy, patience, and support.

And to you, the reader, walking through your own initiations with courage, curiosity, and care, your journey is the reason this book exists. May it serve not just as a book, but as a companion, a mirror, and a reminder.

For permissions or inquiries, contact:
deepshikhasirohi@gmail.com

Printed in India

ISBN: 978-81-980001-9-4

Published with DK FILMS LLP

Dedication

For the versions of us who thought survival was enough.
And for the ones who are ready to live.

TABLE OF CONTENTS

AWAKENING

INTRODUCTION

THE BOOK I NEEDED

Let me break the news for you.

You've been doing everything right. School, job, marriage, house, kids, bills, festivals, smiles for the family album. Check, check, check. You're the model citizen of the life you were told to build.

But tell me, why does it still feel hollow?

Because somewhere between all the achievements, you lost the ability to feel alive. You're scrolling through Instagram at midnight, hypnotized by people who look like they've cracked life's code, beach houses, Bali sunsets, glowing faces. And you whisper to yourself: maybe they just work harder, maybe they're built differently.

Here's the uncomfortable truth: they're not. The happiest people you meet aren't killing themselves with hustle. They've simply stepped off the treadmill you're still running on.

And hustle, let's stop glorifying it, is survival theater. It's running in place, drenched in sweat, clapping for yourself while quietly dying inside.

The Masks We Wear Without Knowing

Think of the last family gathering. You were laughing at the right jokes, complimenting the right outfits, balancing a plate in one hand and expectations in the other. From the outside, you were the picture of stability. Inside? You felt like a cardboard cutout of yourself.

Then came that one remark, an aunt questioning your choices, a colleague mocking your efforts, a sibling comparing you to someone else, and suddenly your whole worth collapsed.

Why? Because you've been living under a contract you never signed: conditional love. Be the good kid. Be the achiever. Be the caretaker. Wear the mask, and maybe you'll be accepted.

Here's the danger no one told you: wear the mask long enough and you forget it's there. You become an actor in a play you never auditioned for.

The Everyday Drama

Maybe for you it wasn't just the hustle. Maybe it was the relationship that broke you.

Like Rhea. She spent three years with a man who lied, cheated, and made her question her worth. Everyone told her the same thing: *"At least you're not alone. Better this than being single at your age."* So she stayed. She told herself he had potential, that maybe he would change, that this must be what love is supposed to feel like.

But here's the truth: she didn't stay because she liked the drama or because she didn't know what she actually wanted in a relationship. She stayed because she was more afraid of being abandoned than of being mistreated. She stayed because somewhere deep inside, a younger version of her still believed that love is something one can earn by holding on tight, even if holding on is breaking you.

And isn't that what so many of us do? We don't question the roots of our choices, we only blame ourselves in the moment. *"I was so stupid. Why did I waste years?"* But stupidity isn't the problem. Conditioning is. We were taught that being accepted, even poorly, is safer than being alone. So we survive the relationship instead of living it.

Now, when we swap out the relationship for a job, the story barely changes.

During my frequent visits to the neighbourhood grocery store, I used to frequently exchange greetings with a guy who stayed in the same apartment as me. One evening, I forgot my wallet at home and somehow I wasn't able to pay online due to technical issues. That time, he paid on my behalf that day and asked me to return the money later. I got to know that his name was Arjun. We walked home together that day and he was a very sweet guy to say the least. We got along as friends and he shared his story with me. On paper, he had the dream job: multinational company, decent pay, weekends off. Yet every morning, his alarm felt like a death sentence. Ever since I started knowing him, I saw him dragging himself through traffic. He used to sit under harsh fluorescent lights, and counted hours like a prisoner scratching marks on the wall. Everyone told him: *"Work is supposed to suck. That's why they call it work."* Or: *"You should be grateful, you're earning well, there are people with nothing."* So he stayed. He convinced himself the dread in his chest was normal. He told himself he was lucky.

But here's the truth: he didn't stay because he loved the job. He stayed because he had been taught that security matters more than joy. He stayed because childhood drilled into him that sacrifice is noble and rest is laziness. He stayed because he didn't believe he had permission to dream outside the script. He shifted to another city after a year or so, and I sometimes wonder how he must be now.

And isn't that what so many of us do? We hate Mondays, we live for weekends, we pray for holidays, but we never stop to ask *why we built a life we constantly need an escape from.* We choose to run away to stop having to face the issues we see ourselves falling into. We blame the boss, the workload, the deadlines, without questioning the deeper root: that somewhere deep down, we're terrified to risk stability for fulfillment. We talk about Monday blues as if it's just for the ones who are corporate slaves, or work a 9 to 5 job or a student. But in reality, it is a menace to even a stay-at-home wife or mother. Families, the most sacred, are the most suffocating stage of all.

They have to dutifully start prepping for the working members of the family from sunrise. In fact, they do not even get a weekly off. Is it not an irony?

So we focus on surviving the job instead of living a life. Everyone around us is just running in survival mode.

Now let me share a little something about Meera, an office colleague from my last job. At every family dinner, she played her role perfectly, smiling, serving, listening. She was that chirpy, bubbly girl whom we all used to love hanging around during college or office. Yet, something changed in her after she got married. She tried to share but whenever she tried to voice an opinion, someone shut her down. *"Don't answer back, it's disrespectful."* Or: *"You're too sensitive, it was just a joke."*

So she stayed quiet. She laughed at comments that cut her. She swallowed her frustration, telling herself: *"That's how families are. Elders can say what they want. It's better to keep the peace."*

But here's the truth: she didn't stay silent because she agreed. She stayed silent because she had been taught that harmony is more important than honesty. She stayed silent because she grew up believing her worth depended on pleasing others, not on honoring herself. She stayed silent because childhood had wired her nervous system to equate love with obedience.

And isn't that what so many of us do? We bite our tongues at the dinner table, nod along in the office, force a smile when we're boiling inside, then go to bed restless, replaying the things we wish we'd said. We blame the people around us for silencing us, but we don't question the deeper script: that somewhere deep down, we still believe approval is safer than truth.

The Game Of Judgment

Now let's flip the mirror. When you judge others, it's not because you're cruel, it's because judgment is easier than honesty.

- See someone meditating in the park on a Tuesday morning? "Must be lazy."
- See a dancer earning a living through her body? "Not a real career."
- See a friend resting when you're still grinding? "Irresponsible."
- See a cousin start a business with family money? "Nepo kid, of course they succeed."

Truth? These reactions aren't about them. They're about you. Carl Jung had it right: what irritates us in others is really pointing us back to ourselves.

When you roll your eyes at rest, maybe it's because you've

never been allowed to rest. When you mock success, maybe it's because you've never been free to pursue what you love. When you scoff at healing, maybe it's because you're terrified of what you'll find when you stop numbing yourself with busyness.

We don't judge because others are wrong. We judge because their freedom of choice makes us uncomfortable. Anything that seems out of our comfort zone or that does not align with what we have been conditioned to believe as normal or sane, frightens us; making us despise it.

And that exactly is why we need to awaken ourselves from the cocoon we are made to believe as the entire world. We need to awaken and understand that something extremely basic as free pursuit has been alien to us.

Awakening Isn't A Luxury

Awakening isn't about floating in the Himalayas, chanting mantras with your phone turned off. Awakening is looking at your daily clichés and realizing:

- "Work is supposed to suck" is a lie.
- "Better to be in a bad relationship than be alone" is a trap.
- "Family respect means silencing yourself" is generational conditioning.

Awakening isn't luxury, it's survival of the soul. Because

if you don't awaken, you'll keep smiling at dinner while feeling like a ghost at your own table. You'll keep hustling, judging, scrolling, numbing, until you forget who you are.

And maybe this will shock you: the life you long for doesn't begin after the promotion, after the loans, after the kids grow up. It begins here. In the messy middle. Beneath the masks.

So let me ask you bluntly: when was the last time you felt like *yourself*, not the employee, not the parent, not the achiever, not the caretaker, but you?

If your answer is "I don't remember," good. That's where we start.

This book isn't a manual. It's not five steps to instant bliss. It's a companion. A mirror. A conversation. Something that will guide you, be your best friend and walk with you hand in hand as you navigate through life's various turns and routes.And it begins with the first mask you ever wore:
The mask of the Good Kid.

CHAPTER 1: THE ILLUSION OF IDENTITY

THE FIRST MASK: THE GOOD KID

From a young age, we learn to wear masks that society encourages us to adopt. One of the earliest and often most influential is that of the "Good Kid." This role comes with an intricate set of expectations: be obedient, please others, and never rock the boat. We internalize the idea that niceness equates to worthiness. Every compliment for being well-behaved reinforces this belief, making it harder to explore who we are beneath the surface.

As children, we often learn that our value comes from meeting others' expectations. We absorb messages from parents, teachers, and peers that emphasize compliance over authenticity. The "Good Kid" mask becomes the armor that shields us from disapproval. Yet with every fake smile and forced agreement to avoid friction, we quietly disconnect from our true selves.

Pause for a moment.
Can you recall a time when you felt praised for being

agreeable, not honest?

Perhaps you recognize moments in your own life where you felt compelled to fit into this mold. Did you ever silence your opinions in class or hold back creativity to avoid standing out?

Remember the many days when you had an opinion to share during the group discussions at school, but never had the courage to. Was it not because you had the fear of being singled out? Not because you were wrong, but because you had a different mindset and opinion than what was generally taught and expected from you. You weren't general or basic. You were unique. And rather than being proud of having an intelligent opinion, you were made to feel bad and keep mum. Or rather you thought it was best to be silent. You yourself started abandoning the self whom you should have embraced the most.

This self-abandonment isn't just a childhood phase; it often extends into adulthood, shaping who we think we need to be.

The fear of disappointing others can be paralyzing, leading us to question our desires and values.

By embracing the "Good Kid" persona, we often forfeit the opportunity to explore our own dreams. Our desires get tangled in the pursuit of approval, pulling us into a life dictated by outside forces. We grow accustomed to living for others often at the cost of our own clarity and joy.

As we transition into adulthood, the stakes rise. Many of us adopt the identity of the "Achiever" , a performance driven by the desire for love and approval. We equate our worth with output, believing that success translates into acceptance. The pursuit of achievement becomes our emotional currency in a world that conditions us to earn belonging.

In striving for excellence, we become like high-performing machines. Whether through grades, promotions, or perfection, we chase goals aligned with societal ideals. The pressure can be overwhelming, as we fear that falling short might mean we no longer matter.

Consider the times you stayed late at work to impress your boss or chose career progress over personal connection. That hunger for validation can be mistaken for ambition but underneath, it often reveals an unmet need to feel seen and safe. And while being celebrated can feel empowering, the high is temporary. Often, the applause fades, and we're left with a quiet emptiness we don't know how to fill.

Over time, the performance takes its toll. As we pour energy into proving ourselves, we neglect our inner world. We excuse our discomfort with productivity and disconnect from what we truly want or feel. The more we chase validation, the more we lose ourselves.

Social and family dynamics only complicate this. We're conditioned to prioritize belonging over authenticity to stay agreeable instead of honest. This inner tension shows up as anxiety, dissatisfaction, and a sense of being emotionally unmoored.

Think about a moment when you followed expectations, even though your gut said no. Maybe it was a job, a relationship, or a major life decision. Did you convince yourself that staying quiet was safer even if it meant losing a piece of yourself?

I remember a time when I prided myself on being everywhere, doing everything. I was juggling two demanding jobs, freelance projects, family obligations exhausted but convinced that busyness proved my worth. Every new task became an emotional investment. I undervalued my work, undercharged, and over-delivered because I didn't believe I had the right to ask for more. I thought, "If I just do this perfectly, maybe I'll finally be recognized." Now you are giving due credit to the mask you wore as the good kid. You are living the lie now. You have now started giving yourself tasks, just for the sake of experiencing an outer feeling of feeling worthy, disregarding your inner struggles and fear. You just want to feel comfortable, even if that means misaligning yourself from your soul purpose.

But under the surface, I was unraveling. A single sentence of feedback "This isn't working" could dismantle me. It wasn't about the work. It was the fact that my worth was completely entangled with other people's approval. I wasn't just working, I was performing, hoping to earn my place.

Eventually, I began losing opportunities not because I lacked skill, but because I was disappearing from myself. I was let go from roles I had poured everything into, not due to incompetence, but because I was mentally and emotionally absent. I was living in survival mode: over-caring, over-efforting, overcompensating for a gnawing discontent.

This pattern seeped into my relationships, too. I clung to partners and routines not out of love, but out of fear, fear of silence, of uncertainty, of being alone with my unmet self. When we stay in what distracts us, we avoid what might heal us.

Even in the comfort of home, I noticed myself moving mechanically, always returning to the kitchen, cooking, cleaning, serving not from joy, but out of habit. It wasn't there. It was a performance, based on an unspoken rule I'd never paused to question.

Until one day, my body said "enough."
My spirit cracked open.
And all that I had been carrying began to fall apart.

It took breakdowns, losses, and burnout to finally hear the voice inside me say:

You are out of alignment.
You are worthy even when you're not performing.

For years, I believed struggle was the currency of growth. But true healing didn't come through pushing; it came through presence. Through honesty. Through the simple, radical act of returning to myself.

And in that return, the masks began to slip.

What We Think Is Love

Compounding our struggles is a quiet, often painful

confusion between **love and control**. Many of us grow up equating love with adherence to expectations, falling into subtle but persistent patterns of **disguised possessiveness**.
How often do we hear phrases like, *"I only want what's best for you,"* when underneath, there's an unspoken condition:

"...as long as it aligns with what I believe is right."

Love, in its truest form, should create space for freedom, individuality, and self-expression. And yet, it often shows up as **pressure to conform** to someone else's ideals. In our eagerness to protect our relationships or preserve harmony, we may begin to **sacrifice our authenticity**, allowing others' values to shape our sense of worth.

This dynamic can take many forms.

Imagine a partner who encourages you to choose a safe, conventional career path over your deeper passion. On the surface, it may seem caring grounded in a desire to ensure your stability. But slowly, that pressure may push you to suppress your creative instincts. You begin to question your desires. You choose practicality over passion, not because it feels right, but because someone else's comfort depends on it.

Parents often carry similar expectations. A child who chooses to study art or philosophy instead of business or engineering may encounter quiet disappointment even if the love remains. That disappointment, though subtle, leaves a mark. It can sow seeds of inadequacy, whispering that love is not unconditional after all but tied to how closely we follow a prescribed path.

Even friendships can reflect this pattern. A close friend might nudge you toward a certain lifestyle, group, or way of being not out of malice, but because your individuality might disrupt the unspoken contract of familiarity. Over time, these influences lead us to internalize the belief that *to belong is to bend.*

These behaviors often operate under the banner of care, but they're built on a foundation of **expectation and subtle control**. Over time, the desire to be accepted begins to collide with the need to be whole. This inner conflict grows quietly, often showing up as anxiety, fatigue, or a vague sense of emotional disconnection.

Navigating this tension requires us to ask hard questions.
What kind of love am I receiving?
Is it love that nurtures my individuality or one that quietly asks me to trade it in?

True love invites us into expansion. It welcomes evolution, creativity, even disagreement. It allows us to grow into ourselves, not just into what others feel comfortable with. Recognizing when care turns into control is a radical act of self-preservation and a doorway to more honest relationships.

In contrast, many of us spend years molding ourselves into roles: the selfless partner, the high-functioning employee, the dutiful child. These identities may appear noble, even admired. But often, they're performances rooted in the fear of disconnection. They offer the illusion of closeness while quietly silencing the voice within.

Breaking free from these roles doesn't mean abandoning

our relationships, it means showing up in them more fully. And this takes courage. Love should be expansive enough to hold your truth, not just your compliance.

Still, many of us remain stuck in a loop of pleasing and performing, seeking validation inside boundaries that quietly **restrict our spirit**. The longer we stay, the more we begin to mistake self-sacrifice for love.

Then comes the moment of quiet reckoning.
The realization that we've been **performing identities** not to thrive, but to be accepted.
We look around and wonder: *"Is this who I am, or who I've needed to be to feel safe?"*

That moment is sacred. It's uncomfortable. It may come after burnout, grief, heartbreak, or a subtle breaking down of everything we thought was "working." But from that crumbling, a deeper truth emerges.

We begin to feel the weight of **identity fatigue, a tiredness** that has nothing to do with our to-do list and everything to do with our detachment from self.
We peel back the mask and whisper: *"Who am I without this?"*

Reclaiming authenticity is not a clean, linear process. It's often slow.
You might resist it.
You might backtrack.
You might miss the old mask it once kept you safe.
But the further you walk toward your truth, the more the mask stops fitting.

Yes, there will be doubt.

Yes, the world might push back.
But there's also an inner voice, once quiet, now growing louder:
You are allowed to be fully yourself even if it disrupts the script others have written for you.

This awakening isn't the end, it's the beginning.
The beginning of a life that feels **real**.
The beginning of relationships built on freedom, not fear.
The beginning of love that doesn't require performance, only presence.

As we explore the illusion of identity, we start to unravel the threads of conditioning that have held us together but also held us back. This unraveling is not a loss. It's a return.

The return to who we were before we were taught to be something else.

CHAPTER 2: SOUL CONDITIONING & BELIEF SYSTEMS

The masks we wear don't just appear in childhood. They are echoes of something older, stitched into us long before we learned to spell our names. The "Good Kid" mask from the last chapter is one expression of a survival story that has been unfolding for thousands of years.

Picture yourself not in your family home, but by a fire in the middle of a vast wilderness. The year is not 2025, but 25,000 BCE. There are no locked doors, no supermarkets, no 24-hour helplines. If you have food, it's because someone hunted or foraged that day. If you are warm, it's because someone kept the fire burning through the night.

In that world, belonging was not optional. It was survival. To be cast out from the tribe wasn't merely sad or embarrassing; it was a death sentence. Alone, you couldn't fend off predators or gather enough food. Alone, you froze, starved, or disappeared.

That's why the need to belong isn't just emotional fluff. It's biology. Our nervous systems evolved to treat rejection as a threat on par with physical danger. When someone raises an eyebrow at you in a meeting, when your partner withdraws into silence, when a friend doesn't return your call your chest tightens, your stomach flips, and your mind races. You're not imagining the intensity of that reaction. Your body thinks exile is coming.

Even today, research shows that the brain processes social rejection much like physical pain. The sting of being left out activates the same neural pathways as breaking a bone. Your body doesn't know the difference between being mocked by a sibling at the dinner table and being abandoned by the campfire. Both feel like survival is at risk.

This is why belonging feels so essential, even when we tell ourselves it shouldn't matter. It explains why you can accomplish everything "right" : the job, the family, the bills paid on time and still crumble at one cutting remark. It's not weakness; it's wiring.
And it's why so many of our so-called personality traits are really survival strategies dressed up for modern life.

The silence you keep when you want to speak? That's camouflage, the ancient instinct to avoid conflict with stronger tribe members. The overachieving that drives you to exhaustion? That's resource-gathering, proof to the group that you're valuable enough to keep. The endless people-pleasing? That's peacemaking, an old tactic to prevent fights that could fracture the tribe. We call it anxiety, perfectionism, or "being responsible." But beneath those labels is an ancient nervous system still doing its job: keeping you safe from exile.

This is what I mean by *soul conditioning*. It's the survival script passed down not just by your parents, but by human history itself. A script written in your very biology, convincing you that safety comes not from authenticity, but from adaptation.

The trouble is, what once saved us now suffocates us. We no longer live in caves. The tribe will not starve if we rest. The wolves are not waiting outside the door. Yet our bodies still act as if one wrong move means we'll be left out in the cold.

And so, without realizing it, we keep living by rules written for another time.

From Survival to Family Conditioning

If ancient humanity gave us the instinct that belonging is survival, childhood gave us the manual on *how to belong*.

As a child, you didn't just learn language or math, you learned what it takes to stay safe in your particular "tribe," your family. And just like your ancestors, you adapted. You watched, listened, absorbed, and adjusted. Not consciously, but through the deepest intelligence of the nervous system.

Children are sponges. They don't only absorb words; they absorb moods, silences, sighs, and the subtle changes in the air when a parent is angry or withdrawn. You inherited not just your family's stories, but their emotional weather.

When your mother broke down behind a closed door but returned to the dinner table smiling, you learned that emotions should be hidden and that vulnerability

threatens harmony.
When your father scoffed at your curiosity, you learned that silence is safer than asking.

When your parents stayed in a loveless marriage for "duty," you absorbed the belief that love is endurance, not joy. No one ever told you these things directly. They seeped into you through tone, gesture, avoidance, and repetition. A curriculum not written in textbooks but etched in your body. Psychologists call this *implicit learning.* It's the way we unconsciously internalize patterns that no one spells out. By the time you're grown, these patterns feel like second nature.

You don't question them, because questioning would have risked belonging when you were small. Think back: were you praised for being quiet, obedient, or "easy"? Did you notice that love arrived when you were helpful, but disappeared when you showed anger or need? Did you learn to perform always smiling, always achieving to secure approval? That wasn't random. It was your nervous system updating the ancient survival script for your unique family environment. If belonging equaled survival, then your role whether caretaker, achiever, peacemaker, or silent one became the mask that guaranteed you wouldn't be cast out.
But here's the cost: what kept you safe as a child can become your prison as an adult.
You grow into someone who hides pain with a smile, who swallows curiosity, who believes love is a heavy duty rather than a free exchange. And because these adaptations run so deep, you don't even recognize them as adaptations. You call them "just the way I am."
But are they?

What if your "I'm fine" smile is camouflage, not authenticity?
What if your perfectionism is proof-seeking, not personality?
What if your endless caretaking is fear of rejection, not love?
The nervous system doesn't distinguish between the campfire of 25,000 BCE and the dinner table of your childhood. In both, the message was the same: adapt or be left behind.

The Myth Of "This Is Just Who I Am"

Here's the trap: when you repeat a survival pattern long enough, it stops feeling like a choice. It feels like identity.
Take busyness. So many of us introduce ourselves with a sigh: *"I'm just the kind of person who can't sit still."* But where did that come from? Perhaps you grew up in a household where stillness was shamed, where a parent equated rest with laziness. Maybe you heard, *"If you've got time to lean, you've got time to clean."* Your nervous system learned early: being busy equals being safe, valuable, and accepted. So now, even on vacation, you struggle to sit by the pool without your mind racing toward the next task. It isn't your nature, it's conditioning.
Or think about self-sacrifice. Many women in particular carry the belief: *"I'm just someone who puts others first."* But scratch beneath the surface and you'll find generations of survival etched into that script. Your grandmother may have learned that her worth came from endurance, that her marriage, her children, her family's reputation all depended on her ability to bend. She passed that on, not through lectures, but through her

silence, her compliance, her careful swallowing of desire. Her daughter took the same and wore it on her head as a crown. And then comes you, her daughter. So you grow up believing that putting others first is noble. But nobility is only half the truth. The other half is fear, the fear that saying no, prioritizing yourself, will fracture the belonging your nervous system equates with survival. It then just becomes another cyclic pattern that's just hard to break.

Then there's achievement. How often do we hear people proudly identify as "perfectionists," as if it's a badge of honor? But perfectionism is rarely about standards, it's about safety. Perhaps as a child, love and attention arrived only when you excelled. A high grade brought a smile, while mistakes drew criticism or shame. Your nervous system registered the pattern: *perform to be valued, achieve to be loved.* Now, as an adult, every project, every email, every interaction carries that invisible weight: if I don't do this flawlessly, I will lose connection. And so achievement hardens into identity.

And then there's silence. Some people insist, *"I'm just not confrontational. I avoid conflict."* But avoidance is not personality, it's protection. Maybe you grew up in a home where speaking your mind sparked rage, withdrawal, or punishment. Your nervous system drew the lesson: silence keeps me safe. Now, as an adult, you bite your tongue, even when your heart pounds with unsaid truths. Not because silence is your authentic voice, but because silence once saved you.

Think of a child who becomes the "responsible one." At first, it's survival: maybe love or attention only arrived when they carried the load, so they learned to equate responsibility with safety. By adulthood, that role has fused with identity. She doesn't just do things responsibly but she believes she *is* responsible for herself. To drop the mask feels like dropping her entire self. The good kid in them still craves to be seen through the small things of life. She still keeps her mask on, even if that means being on survival mode all the time.

Or take the one who learns to be invisible. Maybe in their household, blending in kept them safe from criticism or violence. As an adult, they say, "Oh, I'm shy. I don't like attention." But what if shyness isn't personality at all, but camouflage? What if it's the nervous system still trying to keep them hidden from danger that no longer exists?

This is why self-discovery feels so unsettling. To question the roles we've played can feel like dismantling our very identity. If I'm not the achiever, the helper, the good one then who am I?

The truth is, you are not your adaptations. You are not your masks. Those traits were intelligent responses to your environment, but they are not the essence of you.

Even science supports this. Studies on neuroplasticity show that the brain rewires itself constantly. Habits and identities we cling to are not fixed. They are pathways reinforced by repetition. Just because you've always been the "caretaker" doesn't mean that's all you are. Just because you've always stayed silent doesn't mean your voice isn't waiting beneath the surface.

Here's the paradox: the very behaviors that once ensured belonging are now the ones that keep you disconnected from yourself. They protected you from rejection, but they also cost you authenticity.

It's not that the roles were wrong. They were necessary once. But clinging to them now is like insisting on carrying an umbrella indoors. The tool is outdated. The rain has stopped.

So when you catch yourself saying, "That's just who I am," pause. Ask: is it really? Or is it who you had to be to stay safe?

Because the line between adaptation and identity is thinner than we think.

Cultural & Gender Scripts

The survival strategies that kept our ancestors alive did not stay in caves or family homes. They grew into entire cultural systems. With each generation, what was once a survival necessity was passed down as tradition, morality, and identity.

Let's take women first.

For much of history, a woman's survival depended not on her individuality, but on her compliance. She often had no independent income, no legal ownership of land, and limited freedom of choice. Safety was tied to family, marriage, and reputation. To ensure protection, women learned to prioritize others over themselves, to silence their own desires, and to maintain harmony at all costs.

These were not just personality quirks; they were survival tactics.

Over time, those tactics hardened into cultural ideals. We began to celebrate women as selfless nurturers, obedient daughters, and patient wives. Words like *sacrificial, accommodating, modest* became compliments. Generations later, many women still carry this script, even when their survival no longer depends on it. They cook when they're exhausted, apologize for taking up space, or smile when they want to scream not because they are naturally submissive, but because their nervous systems echo the survival patterns of those who came before them.

When we talk of men, we should remember that for centuries, they were tasked with securing food, defending territory, and ensuring the family's survival in often hostile environments. In that context, emotions were not a luxury, they were a liability. A man who froze in fear during battle, or admitted exhaustion while farming, risked more than embarrassment; he risked the survival of his kin. And so stoic became a virtue. Work became an identity. Productivity became proof of manhood. They weren't given the 'luxury' to be vulnerable. They always had to keep themselves strong and stoic, not showing emotions.

This is why, even today, so many men equate vulnerability with weakness. They believe their value lies in their ability to produce, provide, and endure. When they stop working, or admit fragility, it feels not like rest, it feels like erasure. Again, this isn't natural masculinity; it's survival conditioning that has calcified into culture.

Then there are the collective myths around money and productivity. Imagine your grandparents living through war, famine, or displacement. For them, scarcity was not abstract; it was reality. Every coin mattered, every hour of labor could mean the difference between hunger and survival. Rest was dangerous. Spending was reckless. Debt was shameful. Wealth was often viewed with suspicion, because it created envy and conflict in small, struggling communities.

These experiences solidified into cultural proverbs and household mantras:

- *"Money doesn't grow on trees."*
- *"Idle hands are the devil's workshop."*
- *"A good life is one of sacrifice."*

You may still hear echoes of these today, tucked into the voices of your parents or the tone of your elders. And without questioning, you carry them forward. You work even when exhausted, save even when secure, hustle even when you don't need to. Not because the wolf is at your door but because your nervous system has been trained to believe that pausing means danger.

The tragedy is that when these survival codes become cultural scripts, they no longer feel optional. They feel like morality.

We have made some definitions that society deems necessary. Some things that make everything seem to fall in place. A woman who rests is lazy. A man who cries is weak. A person who questions tradition is ungrateful. Productivity is praised as virtue; exhaustion is framed as devotion.

But strip back the layers, and what are these really? They are outdated instructions rules written for different times, passed down so many times that they began to look like the truth.

That's why it's so hard to challenge them. You're not just confronting a personal habit; you're confronting centuries of conditioning disguised as culture.

The Cost Of Outdated Scripts

The trouble with survival codes is not that they were wrong. It's that they are outdated. Our nervous systems still behave as if exile is around the corner, even though the danger has long passed. What once kept us alive now keeps us small. We often meet women who cannot let themselves rest. Their bodies ache, their minds are foggy, yet they keep pushing because they've been taught that pausing makes them lazy.

This script is rarely personal. It comes from generations who had no choice but to work themselves sick just to put food on the table. The problem is, today the refrigerator may be full, the bills may be paid, and still their nervous systems treat rest as a threat. The result is burnout, insomnia, and a gnawing sense of never being "enough." We also meet men who define themselves entirely by work. They provide, they hustle, they achieve, but behind the surface is a hollowness. Their identity is tied so tightly to productivity that stopping feels like disappearing. Vulnerability feels dangerous, joy feels like indulgence, and presence feels impossible. This isn't because they are flawed, it's because they inherited the script that value equals output.And it's not only men and women in isolation. Across cultures, we encounter people who confuse exhaustion with devotion, who call silence "peace" even when it is suppression, who call self-sacrifice "love" even when it erases the self, who call busyness "purpose" even when it's avoidance.

The cost of these outdated scripts is profound.

Outwardly, lives look like successful houses, jobs, families, routines. Inwardly, there is restlessness, hollowness, and often, a quiet grief. By midlife, this grief gets harder to ignore. The body begins to protest through anxiety, fatigue, mood swings, even unexplained illnesses. The soul protests too, in dissatisfaction that no promotion, vacation, or purchase can fix.

This is not a weakness. It is awakening. The nervous system, after decades of carrying masks that no longer fit, starts to whisper: *enough.*

And beneath all the exhaustion lies perhaps the deepest cost: we forget who we are. We meet countless people who have worn their roles so faithfully, the caretaker, the achiever, the peacemaker that they can no longer distinguish between the mask and themselves. The irony is painful. What began as strategies to protect belonging now rob us of authenticity, the very essence of real belonging. So many carry this secret fatigue. They go to bed with the dull ache of a life that looks good on paper but feels hollow at the core. They scroll, envy the freedom of others, and then shame themselves for wanting more.

But that ache is not a failure. It's not proof that something is wrong with you. It's proof that the survival code has run its course.

The rules you inherited were brilliant once. They saved lives. But they were never meant to become prisons.

Beyond Conditioning: The Inheritance We Never Chose

By now it's clear: so much of what we call *"personality"* is not identity, but adaptation. We bend, we achieve, we silence, we serve all in the name of belonging. And while these masks once kept us safe, they also keep us distant from ourselves. But here is the haunting truth: not all of this conditioning even belongs to you.

When we trace the threads of our survival scripts, they lead us backward through our own memories, into the lives of those who came before us. Your mother's silence at the dinner table, your father's relentless work ethic, your grandmother's self-sacrifice - these were not inventions of their character. They, too, were following scripts written long before them. This is nothing but conditioning. Something we need to break from, break through and come out woke.

A woman who never spoke her desires may have carried the survival code of her time, when a single act of defiance could mean abandonment or ruin.

A man who drowned himself in work may have been echoing his father, who knew hunger so intimately that rest felt unsafe.
Entire families endured wars, migrations, poverty, dislocation and what they couldn't process, they passed down. Not through conscious teaching, but through nervous systems, emotional climates, and the unspoken rules of the home.

This is why you can live in comfort yet carry the anxiety of scarcity. Why can you grow up in peace yet tremble at conflict? Why can you be loved yet still feel unworthy?
Because sometimes, the ache inside you is not yours. It is an echo.

Psychologists call this *intergenerational transmission of trauma.* Neuroscientists have found that stress can literally alter genetic expression, priming the next generation for vigilance even if the threat is gone. In simpler terms: the body remembers what the mind cannot. So when you find yourself exhausted by self-sacrifice, terrified of failure, unable to rest pause before you call it weakness. Ask instead: *Whose survival story am I reenacting?*
Maybe the pressure to endure is your grandmother's voice, still alive in your nervous system. Maybe the drive to overwork is your father's scarcity, passed to you like heirloom furniture. Maybe your fear of being "too much" is the echo of generations of women taught to shrink.

What feels like *your flaw* may actually be *your inheritance.*

And here lies the possibility that can take your breath away: if it was inherited, it can be released. The pain you carry is not proof that you are broken. It is proof that you are human, woven into a lineage that endured. And now, for the first time, you have the awareness and the freedom to ask: *Do I want to continue carrying this, or does it end with me?* This is where awakening deepens. Because true alignment does not only mean peeling off your own masks, it also means honoring the burdens you were handed and daring to set them down. Not with bitterness. With reverence. With gratitude for those who endured so you could exist. And with courage to live differently, so those who come after you will not inherit the same chains. This is where the story shifts from survival to liberation. And it begins with recognizing the wounds that aren't ours.

CHAPTER 3: THE WEIGHT OF WOUNDS THAT AREN'T OURS

THE MISALIGNMENT WHISPER

By the time we arrive in midlife, most of us know how to keep life running. We pay bills, raise children, hold down jobs, and maintain appearances. We've built routines, identities, and roles we can perform almost without thinking. On the outside, it looks like stability. On the inside, something doesn't sit right.

It's rarely dramatic. Not always a collapse or a crisis. Often, it shows up as a quiet gnawing fatigue that doesn't lift, joy that feels muted, a restlessness that hums beneath even our proudest accomplishments. We might say we're tired, uninspired, confused, or "just not ourselves." But beneath those vague words is a deeper truth: something in us has gone out of alignment.

Alignment is not about having a perfect life. It's not about smooth days or constant positivity. Alignment is when your outer choices flow from your inner truth. It's when

what you say, do, and give matches what you actually want and feel. Misalignment, then, is the gap between the life you perform and the life you long for.
Wounds often create that gap.
Wounds that whisper: *Don't rest, you'll be left behind.*
Wounds that echo: *Don't speak, you'll be shamed.*
Wounds that insist: *Earn more, prove more, hold more, then you'll be safe.*

And here's the difficult part: many of these wounds are not the scars of our own mistakes or failures. They are inheritances emotional imprints from the families and cultures that raised us.

This is why misalignment feels confusing. On paper, we're doing everything "right." But the script we're following may not even be ours. It's a script shaped by the pain and survival strategies of those who came before us. The result is a life that looks full but feels hollow. A life that works but doesn't feel alive.

And so the whisper grows louder: *Whose wounds am I carrying? Whose voice is shaping my choices?*

The Nature Of Wounds

When people hear the word *wound*, they often imagine something dramatic: abuse, abandonment, tragedy. But many of the wounds that shape us are far quieter. They don't announce themselves with chaos; they slip into us through small, repeated moments that slowly fracture our sense of self.
Let's take an example. A wound can form in the silence

after you shared a dream and someone laughed. This might be when you felt that sharing meant having to deal with judgment. OR believing that being vulnerable meant inviting pain.

It can form in the raised eyebrow when you show too much enthusiasm. It can form in the phrase, *"Don't be silly"* or *"You're too sensitive."*

Nothing catastrophic happens. No one calls it trauma. But inside, the nervous system takes note: *This part of me is unsafe. Better hide it.*

Psychologists call these experiences *micro-traumas.* They are small in isolation, but powerful in repetition. Over time, they accumulate into invisible laws that shape our identities. Research from the **Adverse Childhood Experiences (ACE) Study** shows that even subtle forms of neglect or invalidation can have lifelong effects on health, increasing risks for anxiety, depression, autoimmune illness, and even heart disease. The body remembers what the mind tries to dismiss.

And yet, because these wounds are quiet, we rarely honor them. We minimise:

"It wasn't that bad."

"Other people had it worse."

"I turned out fine."

But the truth is, these micro-wounds shape how we show up in the world.

A child told she's "too much" grows into a woman who dims her light in every boardroom, friendship, and love affair.

A boy mocked for crying becomes a man who struggles to let anyone close enough to see him.

A teenager dismissed for dreaming learns to distrust his

own desires, living a life that looks practical but feels empty.

Wounds don't vanish when we grow up. They weave themselves into the fabric of our nervous system. They become filters lenses that bend how we interpret the present. That's why a simple cancelled plan can sting like abandonment, or a small criticism can spiral into shame. The reaction feels bigger than the moment because it's not about the moment. It's about the wound.

And here's the most subtle part: over time, we stop seeing these wounds as wounds at all. We call them *"just who I am."*

- We say, *"I hate conflict,"* when really, conflict once felt unsafe.
- We say, *"I have high standards,"* when really, imperfection once cost us love.
- We say, *"I'm independent,"* when really, needing others once led to disappointment.

The wound hides in plain sight, disguised as identity.

How Wounds Disguise Themselves as Strengths

One of the cleverest tricks of the human psyche is how it disguises wounds as virtues.

We don't walk around announcing, *"I am carrying pain."* Instead, we decorate our wounds, polish them, and present them as personality, as strength, as pride.

The girl who learned that being agreeable kept her safe

grows into a woman admired for her generosity. She always shows up, always says yes, always smooths the rough edges in relationships. People call her dependable. She calls herself caring. In real, she is breaking, struggling to stay alive. But she still carries on wering the mask and hiding it all, just for the sake of feeling belonged. Beneath it all lies a wound that whispers: *If I stop giving, I might stop being loved.*

The boy who once felt helpless in a chaotic home grows into a man who controls every detail of his environment. He is praised for being disciplined, organised, successful. What others see as ambition is often a wound dressed as structure, a nervous system saying: *If I control everything, maybe I'll never feel powerless again.*

The child who learned that emotions were unwelcome grows into an adult who prides themselves on stoicism. They don't cry, don't complain, don't "burden" anyone. Colleagues call them strong. Friends admire their composure. Yet inside, the wound murmurs: *If I show my heart, I'll be shamed or abandoned.*

Even resilience, the quality we often celebrate most, is sometimes a mask. Surviving hardship and pushing forward can look like strength, but it can also be the body's refusal to pause long enough to feel what was lost. The wound hides behind the medal of endurance.

Psychologist Alice Miller wrote: "What is often called a "strong character" is a form of early adaptation to parental needs and expectations." In other words, strength may sometimes be survival in disguise.

This doesn't mean our strengths aren't real. They are. But

when they grow from wounds, they carry a heaviness. They exhaust us, because they are not freely chosen, they are compelled.

That's why the people who appear the strongest often confess, in private, to feeling the most tired. Behind the perfect achievement, the calm smile, the well-managed home, is a nervous system working overtime to hold the mask in place.

The true measure of strength isn't how well we hide our wounds. It's how gently we can begin to face them. One big example that comes to my mind is the recent death of a very famous influencer. Everything in his life seemed picture perfect. Every post screamed happiness or so we thought. But inside he was dying slowly. Until when he finally killed himself, leaving everyone shocked. But there were hints. There were signs. It's just that no one's actually caring enough to see. If at all he saw it himself. If at all he cared the most and made himself seen. He would still be here amongst us. Thriving.

The Echo Effect: Passing Wounds On

One of the hardest truths to face is this: what we don't heal, we hand down. Wounds don't simply vanish with time. They echo. They seep into the way we speak, the choices we make, the love we offer, and the patterns we normalize. What is unprocessed within us finds a way to live on, often without our awareness.

Think of the parents who never learned emotional safety in their own childhood. When their child cries, instead of offering comfort, they say, *"Stop being dramatic."* Not because they don't love their child, but because their own wound of emotional invalidation has never been healed. The cycle repeats: one generation silenced, then the next. Or the father who was taught as a boy that vulnerability is weakness. When his son shows sadness, he dismisses it, hoping to "toughen him up." He doesn't see that he is not strengthening his child; he is passing on the same wound he once carried. He is again repeating the same cycle he has been struggling to break free form. He has taught his son how being vulnerable meant being weak, and how hiding emotions were a man's real strength.

Mothers, too, often pass down their inheritance of endurance. A woman raised to believe love is measured in sacrifice may unintentionally raise her daughter to equate exhaustion with worth. It's transmitted in sighs, in body language, in the way she never rests. The daughter absorbs it silently, and one day wonders why she feels guilty every time she puts her feet up.

This is the echo effect: wounds unspoken but deeply lived. Science has begun to map what families have always intuited: wounds leave imprints not just emotionally, but biologically. **Epigenetic research** has shown that trauma alters how genes are expressed, changing stress responses in children and even grandchildren. Descendants of Holocaust survivors, for instance, often exhibit heightened cortisol levels, even if they never personally experienced war. The body remembers what the mind cannot.

This explains why we sometimes feel the weight of fears or anxieties that don't match our own lived experience, why scarcity haunts people who grew up with enough. Why does the fear of abandonment linger in those who were never left? We may be carrying the emotional fingerprints of wounds from generations before us.

The echo effect is not meant to condemn us, it's meant to awaken us. Because once we see the pattern, we are no longer just inheritors. We become interrupters.

We can choose to say: *It ends here.*

By meeting our wounds with awareness instead of denial, we stop handing them down unconsciously. We give our children, partners, and communities a chance to inherit something different: not silence, not fear, not endless performance but presence, compassion, and truth.

Awareness As Disruption

If wounds are inherited echoes, then awareness is the interruption.

At first glance, awareness seems almost too simple. Notice your reactions? Pause to ask yourself questions? It doesn't sound revolutionary. But the truth is, awareness is one of the most radical forces we have. Because to see clearly is to disrupt centuries of conditioning.

Think of how most of us live: on autopilot. A comment stings, and before we even think, we shrink into silence or flare into anger. A partner forgets something, and we spiral into anxiety. A friend cancels plans, and we feel abandoned. These reactions feel instantaneous, but they are rarely about the present. They are about the past the wound remembering itself.

Awareness interrupts this cycle. Instead of collapsing into the automatic reaction, we pause. We ask: *Why did that hit me so hard? What story am I telling myself? When did I first feel this way?*

These questions don't erase the wound, but they begin to loosen its grip. They take us off autopilot and put us back into choice.

Neuroscience backs this up. Studies using brain imaging show that when we **name an emotion**, the amygdala, the brain's alarm centre, calms down, while the prefrontal cortex, responsible for reasoning and self-regulation, becomes more active. Simply saying, *"I feel shame"* or *"I feel fear"* is enough to shift the brain's chemistry, lowering the charge of the wound.

This is why mindfulness, journaling, and therapy are not luxuries; they are tools of liberation. They help us notice the wound instead of reenacting it. In noticing, we stop unconsciously handing it forward.

Carl Jung once said, *"Until you make the unconscious conscious, it will direct your life and you will call it fate."* Awareness is the moment fate bends.

And it doesn't just shift our own lives, it shifts everything around us. The parent who notices their impulse to dismiss their child's tears may pause and offer comfort instead. The partner who recognises their urge to control may take a breath and soften. The friend who realizes they are over-apologising may finally speak without shrinking.

Small interruptions. Tiny moments of awareness. Yet each one is a thread cut in a pattern that has lasted generations.

This is why awareness matters. Not because it is neat or easy, but because it is disruptive. It is rebellion against silence. It is a revolution against inheritance.

The Grief And The Gift

Awareness changes everything, but it also breaks your heart a little.

Because with every wound you begin to recognize, grief comes too. You grieve the child who swallowed her voice to keep the peace. You grieve the teenager who dimmed his joy to avoid ridicule. You grieve the years spent mistaking exhaustion for love, silence for harmony, and perfection for safety.

This grief is not weakness, it is reverence. It is the honoring of all the versions of you who did the best they could with what they knew.

And here is the gift: the moment you see the wound, you are no longer defined by it.

What once controlled you unconsciously now stands in the light of your awareness. And in that light, you begin to realize these wounds may live in you, but they are not *you*. They are imprints, echoes, survival codes. They may have shaped your path, but they do not own your future.

This is where liberation begins. Because the most profound truth is this: what was passed down through pain can end with you through presence.

But the story doesn't stop here because wounds don't stay quiet. What we do not tend to, they demand of us. They rise to the surface in the form of triggers, moments when the past floods the present, when a comment, a look, or a silence ignites a reaction far bigger than the moment deserves.

If wounds are the roots, triggers are the flare of fire above the ground. They are how the nervous system keeps tugging at us, saying: *Something here still needs your attention.*

To understand our wounds fully, we must learn to listen to our triggers not as enemies, but as messengers.

And that is where we go next.

CHAPTER 4: TRAUMA AND TRIGGERS

When wounds are not recognized and processed, they can evolve into trauma, manifesting as various emotional and psychological struggles. Unaddressed wounds simmer beneath the surface, creating a fertile ground for a range of negative experiences. Aggression often surfaces as a defense mechanism; when we are unable to confront our own pain, we may lash out at others, turning our inner turmoil into outward hostility. Similarly, feelings of guilt or inadequacy can develop when we suppress our wounds, leading to a cycle of self-blame and diminished self-worth.

Depression can also emerge as a heavy cloak that dims our perspective on life. It often stems from our inability to acknowledge and work through our emotional injuries. The weight of unprocessed trauma can lead to a sense of stagnation, making it difficult to find joy or motivation. Fights with those close to us can escalate as unresolved feelings bubble to the surface, where minor disagreements transform into major conflicts, fueled by a history of unexpressed hurt.

Anxiousness serves as another signal that something within us is unresolved. When we don't confront our wounds, the constant worry and fear about the future can take hold, stemming from a deep-seated belief that we are unworthy or unsafe. These feelings may lead us to overreact or withdraw from situations and relationships, reinforcing a cycle of isolation and distress.

Moreover, the way we navigate our relationships is often a reflection of our unhealed wounds. The dynamics we establish with others can reveal a lot about what we need to work on within ourselves. If we find ourselves consistently drawn to toxic relationships, experiencing codependency, or feeling an overwhelming fear of abandonment, these patterns may indicate unresolved trauma that needs to be addressed.

The people we encounter can serve as mirrors, reflecting our own unresolved issues. When we react strongly to someone else's behaviour, it may signify a part of us that we haven't acknowledged or accepted. Challenging interactions can reveal the areas where we need healing and self-discovery. Ultimately, recognizing these patterns is the first step toward making the unconscious conscious.

What Is Trauma, Really?

Trauma is frequently mischaracterised as solely originating from overtly harmful events, such as abuse, violence, or profound loss. However, a more nuanced understanding reveals that trauma can also emerge from emotional neglect and the absence of crucial support. It might look like a parent unable to attune to your needs, leaving you unseen. Or a teacher humiliating you in front of peers, instilling shame. Or a household that celebrated achievement but stifled sadness.

Ultimately, trauma embodies the deep-seated loneliness that arises from not being emotionally recognized or validated.

Because these experiences often go unacknowledged, they can fester within us, leading to the development of coping mechanisms that allow us to function despite the pain. We end up constructing our lives over this unresolved emotional terrain. However, the body retains the memory of these traumas, and our nervous systems remain alert to them, constantly influenced by past experiences.

Triggers Are Teachers

A trigger occurs when our nervous system overreacts to a present situation that bears resemblance to a past trauma we haven't fully processed. The strength of our emotional response is less about the current event and more about its connections to unresolved pain from the past.

For example, if your partner doesn't text back quickly, the upset you feel could be tied to unresolved feelings from childhood experiences of being ignored. Similarly, if a colleague questions your work, it may evoke old wounds related to being overlooked or shamed when you expressed yourself as a child.

When triggers surface, we typically respond in one of two ways: we either react impulsively or suppress our feelings entirely. But what if we allowed ourselves a moment to pause and reflect?

What is this trigger revealing about my internal landscape?

Which part of me is feeling unseen, unheard, or unsafe right now?

Is this pain a familiar echo from my past?

Each trigger acts as a valuable clue, a breadcrumb leading us back to an unresolved aspect of ourselves that longs for acknowledgement and integration, rather than avoidance.

Trauma Responses Are Adaptations

It's common for individuals to feel shame regarding their coping mechanisms. However, it's essential to recognize that every trauma response was once a brilliant survival strategy.

- The Fight response empowered you to resist and protect yourself from being overpowered by others.

- The Flight response offered you the essential space to escape overwhelming situations.

- The Freeze response provided a means of numbing and distancing yourself from unbearable pain.

- The Fawn response made you likeable enough to avoid rejection, criticism, or abuse.

Yet, these adaptive strategies, originally designed as survival tools, often evolve into psychological prisons in adulthood. For example, the achiever may struggle to rest, driven by an incessant need for validation. The helper may find it hard to say no, fearing that unworthiness will surface. The perfectionist can become paralyzed by the fear of failure. Beneath it all lies a nervous system that is still anxiously waiting for the chance to exhale and find peace.

The Ego: Protector, Not Enemy

In many spiritual discussions, the ego often finds itself labelled as the antagonist or the source of our internal strife. However, a more nuanced perspective reveals that the ego functions as a guardian, one that has inadvertently become overly rigid and protective over time. It shapes our identity as a safety mechanism, crafting a facade that shields us from confronting our deepest wounds and vulnerabilities.

Consider the different facets of the ego:

- The Overachiever often emerges as a façade designed to protect against feelings of unworthiness and inadequacy, pushing us to seek validation through success and accomplishments constantly. This relentless drive can lead to burnout and a profound sense of emptiness, as our self-worth becomes inextricably linked to external achievements.

- The Peacemaker, on the other hand, operates out of a fear of conflict and abandonment. By smoothing over disagreements and prioritizing harmony, this aspect of the ego may prevent us from expressing our authentic thoughts and feelings, leading to a build-up of resentment and emotional disconnection.

- The Critic serves as an internal voice that veils the deep-seated shame of not feeling "good enough." This harsh self-judgment can trap us in a cycle of negative self-perception, stunting our growth and stifling our creativity.

- Lastly, the Helper is driven by the belief that love must be earned through self-sacrifice and relentless giving. This mindset can lead to an imbalance in relationships, where our needs and desires are consistently sidelined in favor of others, leaving us feeling depleted and unvalued.

When someone challenges the carefully constructed facade that our ego has created, our reaction often isn't simply a response to that individual; rather, it is a defensive manoeuvre safeguarding us from the fear of exposing our most vulnerable wounds. Recognizing the role of the ego as a protector can foster a more compassionate relationship with ourselves and our histories, allowing us to dismantle its rigidity gradually.

Triggers as Portals

In moments of emotional triggering, our instinct may be to withdraw or retaliate. However, what if we chose instead to pause, breathe, and reflect on these reactions? What if these triggers were invitations rather than obstacles, portals to deeper understanding?

For instance, a woman who experiences overwhelming anxiety when plans change might trace that emotional response back to her upbringing in a chaotic home environment, where inconsistency was synonymous with danger. Her nervous system learns to equate change with threat, leading to disproportionate reactions in adult life.

Similarly, a man who reacts with irritation when corrected might be grappling with an ingrained belief that being wrong equates to unworthiness, an echo of a childhood where mistakes were met with harsh criticism. By examining our triggers through this lens, we invite an opportunity for healing and growth. When we ask ourselves, "What does this reaction reveal about what I learned growing up?" we embark on a path of unlearning, allowing us to rewrite the narratives that have been shaping our lives.

Shadow Work and Projection

Carl Jung famously stated, "Until you make the unconscious conscious, it will direct your life and you will call it fate." The parts of ourselves that we suppress, such as anger, neediness, or vulnerability, do not vanish. Instead, they retreat underground, festering and manifesting through projection onto others.

We may find ourselves judging those we perceive as "too much" for expressing themselves freely, while unconsciously reproaching our own need to suppress our emotions due to past experiences that discouraged such authenticity. We might resent those who openly display emotion; this disdain often stems from our own unprocessed feelings, as we were never afforded the safety to express them.

Additionally, we may accuse others of controlling us, all while rigidly attempting to manage every aspect of our lives to avoid chaos. Shadow work invites us to reclaim these rejected aspects of ourselves, not to act them out impulsively, but to integrate them into our understanding of who we are. It's a journey of acceptance: to acknowledge, "Yes, I can be vulnerable and still be strong."

Integration does not equate to indulging in our wounds. Instead, it requires us to recognize, soothe, and ultimately rewrite the beliefs that once formed out of those painful experiences. This process lays the groundwork for personal growth, authentic relationships, and a deeper connection to our true selves, fostering resilience in our journey towards wholeness.

It's natural to believe that we fully control our choices in relationships, careers, and roles. However, many of us find ourselves acting from our wounds rather than our true selves.

Consider the woman who tends to overgive in her relationships; she might be unwittingly trying to earn the love that once felt so far out of reach with emotionally distant parents. Similarly, the man who hesitates to ask for help may still be carrying the belief that needing others is a sign of weakness. And for the adult who fears conflict, peace may only feel achievable by fading into the background.

These patterns are not rooted in logic; they stem from

deeper emotional imprints. Often, we do not actively choose our behaviors; we repeat them until we become aware of our choices.

When we carry unhealed wounds, it's common to seek in our partners what we didn't receive in childhood, but this often leads us to recreate pain rather than heal it. Our love can sometimes feel like a pull toward the familiar rather than a true connection.

Let's take some examples to understand. For instance, someone who grew up with emotional neglect might find themselves drawn to distant partners, hoping this time they will stay. Those raised by controlling parents may feel safest with partners who take charge, only to find that resentment builds over time. Meanwhile, individuals who had to take care of their own parents might attract emotionally needy partners, mistaking this pattern for love.

These dynamics often operate unconsciously. In our desire to heal, we may recreate our wounds, but without awareness, we risk bleeding into every new relationship.

Many of us turn to our work to soothe unrecognized wounds. The achiever might be chasing the approval they missed as a child, while the perfectionist equates mistakes with shame. The workaholic might be fleeing the discomfort of silence. This is why burnout frequently arises not just from a heavy workload, but also from tying our self-worth to productivity.

When we equate our value with our usefulness, taking time to rest can feel like an unattainable luxury rather than a necessary reprieve. Rest disrupts the ongoing story about our worth.

Our adult identities are often shaped by the pain we've experienced. We might become the strong one, the responsible one, or the cheerful one, not always out of genuine choice but from necessity. Over time, as we embody these roles, we may forget who we are beneath the masks we wear.

Removing these masks can be daunting. We might fear being labelled selfish, lazy, dramatic, or weak, fears that often stem from how we were made to feel when we expressed our needs in the past. Healing doesn't mean becoming someone new; rather, it involves rediscovering who we were before the world around us influenced us.

In psychological terms, this can be called repetition compulsion, the tendency to unconsciously repeat painful dynamics from our early lives in the hope of achieving a different outcome. We might stay in jobs that reflect the authoritarian energy of our childhoods or choose friends who gossip and invalidate us because we were taught to earn connection rather than simply receive it. At times, we even overlook red flags, as the familiarity of pain can feel safer than the uncertainty of joy.

True healing begins when we can interrupt this cycle, not by blaming others, but by acknowledging our role in these patterns and choosing to step away from them. This process of awareness can open the door to liberation and genuine connection.

How Wounds Shape Relationships

Most of our conflicts in relationships stem not from the other person, but from echoes of earlier pain playing out in real time. We often don't fall in love with a person; instead, we fall into a familiar pattern. This pattern mirrors our earliest caregivers, even if that experience was painful. Our nervous system craves familiarity over peace.

A child who had to perform for love may unconsciously be drawn to emotionally unavailable partners, as earning love feels normal to them. Similarly, someone raised in a volatile environment might confuse intensity with passion, mistaking adrenaline for connection.

This isn't a sign of being broken; rather, it indicates that we're attempting to resolve a story that never reached closure. By recreating similar dynamics, we hope that this time someone will stay, choose us, and love the parts of ourselves we had to hide. However, repeating the same story doesn't heal it; awareness does.

When a wound goes unhealed, it acts as a lens through which we perceive the world. We don't see others as they truly are; instead, we view them as threats to our emotional safety. For example:

- If we fear abandonment, we may become hyper-vigilant to any sign of withdrawal.

- If we fear rejection, we may sabotage closeness before others can hurt us.

- If we were criticised constantly, we might become overly defensive or attract partners who perpetuate that internalised criticism.

These behaviors are not faults but protective patterns developed in childhood that now distort our adult relationships.

Relationships do more than fulfill our desires; they reflect our inner wounds. What we admire in others often mirrors what we suppress in ourselves, and what triggers us reflects what we have yet to heal. For instance:

- A partner who sets boundaries might trigger feelings of unworthiness within us.

- A friend's independence can awaken our fears of abandonment.

- A colleague's assertiveness may reflect our own disowned anger.

Instead of viewing relationships purely as sources of happiness or pain, consider seeing them as teachers, sacred spaces that reveal where we still seek freedom.

Without self-awareness, we form connections based on mutual wounding rather than mutual growth. For example:

- The caretaker-rescuer dynamic may appear loving, but it often disguises codependency.

- The critic-victim loop might feel dramatic, but is a re-enactment of unresolved parent-child pain.

- The avoidant-anxious dance may seem romantic, yet it often represents trauma bonding, a painful push-and-pull of unmet needs.

The more we identify our wounds, the less we inflict them on those who did not cause them.

While introspection is vital, healing occurs within relationships. Our wounds were formed through connection, and they can also be healed in connection. When we express a need and it's met, we rewrite the belief that needs are unsafe. When we are vulnerable without being judged, we diminish the hold of shame. When we feel triggered yet are still loved, we learn that we don't have to be perfect to be worthy.

Healing is not about avoiding triggers; instead, it's about building enough self-trust to face them with awareness. It's about allowing the old story to surface and choosing a new one in real-time.

Everyday Triggers That Reveal Soul Conditioning

We don't always notice when we're triggered. Often, it manifests in subtle ways rather than overt expressions like crying or yelling. Sometimes, it appears as a sudden emotional shutdown, a retreat from engagement, or an overwhelming urge to prove oneself. Recognizing these reactions is the crucial first step in healing the deeper wounds that prompted them. Here are some everyday examples that illustrate these triggers:

Someone interrupts you while you're talking

In that moment, you may feel dismissed, as if your thoughts and feelings are not valued. Your chest tightens with a sense of frustration; you might either go quiet out of discomfort or feel compelled to over-explain your point.

Reflect: When did I learn that my voice doesn't matter?

Root Wound: This often stems from a belief that "I must earn space to speak," a mindset usually rooted in experiences of being emotionally overlooked or silenced during childhood.

You receive unexpected feedback

Even if the feedback is constructive and intended to help, your body may react with tension, your heart rate may increase, and you may feel judged or attacked.

Reflect: Why does critique feel like rejection?

Root Wound: This reaction is often tied to perfectionism and a deep-seated fear of failure, which can be linked to childhood experiences where love and acceptance were conditional on "being good" or performing perfectly.

Someone you love doesn't reply to your message

You may find yourself checking your phone repeatedly, your mind racing with anxious thoughts. Questions like, "Did I do something wrong? Are they upset with me?" start spiralling out of control.

Reflect: When did silence feel like punishment?

Root Wound: This response often points to a fear of abandonment or an anxious attachment style, rooted in experiences of inconsistent affection from caregivers during formative years.

You see others succeed in the same field as you

While you genuinely want to feel happy for their success, you find yourself feeling small and unseen, like you're lagging behind in your own journey.

Reflect: What belief do I hold about my own worth or timing?

Root Wound: This feeling is often linked to a scarcity mindset, where comparison masks a deeper belief: "There's not enough love, attention, or success for me," fostering feelings of inadequacy.

Someone sets a boundary with you

You may feel hurt or offended, even when the boundary is expressed kindly. A sense of shame or guilt may wash over you as you contemplate whether you did something wrong.

Reflect: Why does someone else's limit feel like rejection?

Root Wound: This typically reflects ingrained people-pleasing patterns, stemming from the belief that love means self-sacrifice or emotional merging with others.

You make a small mistake

In an instant, panic takes hold; you may find yourself apologizing repeatedly or trying to overcorrect your actions.

Reflect: What do I believe mistakes say about me?

Root Wound: This reaction often originates from

environments where mistakes were met with punishment rather than support, fostering a crippling inner shame and fear of inadequacy.

You feel responsible for someone else's emotions

When someone close to you is upset, you may internalize their feelings, believing it's your responsibility to fix the situation. You slip into "fix-it" mode, often at the expense of your own emotional well-being.

Reflect: When did I learn that my role is to manage others' peace?

Root Wound: This tendency is frequently rooted in codependency and a fawn response, typically arising from homes characterized by emotional volatility or unpredictable caregiving.

You're offered help, and you decline

Even when feeling tired or overwhelmed, you may instinctively say, "No, I'm fine," rejecting offers of assistance.

Reflect: Why does receiving support feel unsafe or weak?

Root Wound: This reaction may be based on hyper-independence, a belief that you need to "be strong" and prove your worth through self-sufficiency, often cultivated in environments that undervalued vulnerability.

Take a moment to notice which of these triggers resonate with you. It's important not to rush into fixing them; approach them with honesty and curiosity. Each trigger represents a doorway, a path leading back to the core of where your soul first learned to armor itself against pain and rejection. Embrace this journey as an opportunity for profound healing and self-discovery.

CHAPTER 5: THE ILLUSION OF HOME

We often hear that home is where love lives, where you feel comfortable and belong, and where you are safe and wanted. But for many people, home becomes the place where they first learn to hide. It turns into an environment where silence is valued, obeying rules is praised, and being honest about your feelings is punished.

In this setting, you learn to hide your true feelings. You become trained to smile while suppressing what you feel. You serve others before you speak for yourself. You start to think that you must erase your own identity to earn love. Instead of a safe place, home can turn into the first stage where you perform for others.

You might not remember when this started. You don't recall when you began to nod instead of saying "no." You don't remember when you prepared a meal, even when you were sick. You carry the uneasy feeling of being watched but never really seen.

When we think of "home," we picture a place. But home

is also a system. It is a structure built on rules you didn't create, roles you didn't choose, and traditions you weren't allowed to question. These ideas shape how you see the world before outside influences come in. Your childhood home defines what is acceptable and what must be hidden.

Yet, we still call this love.

This reflection invites deeper contemplation: Is your perception of home genuinely your own, or is it a derivative of what you inherited? Were you truly loved in the way you needed, or were you simply valued for your utility? As you navigate your adult life, are you still tethered to the unarticulated roles and expectations instilled in you during your childhood? These questions linger, urging a reassessment of what home truly means.

The Home as the First System

Long before you set foot in a classroom, long before you were introduced to the intricate rules of religion, societal norms, or workplace culture, you were already being conditioned within a system called home. This environment shaped your earliest perceptions of authority, who commands the final word in decision-making, whose voice resonates with significance, whose needs are prioritized in times of crisis, and whose concerns are relegated to the background.

In this microcosm of society, the home offered your first lessons on gender roles. You observed the implicit divisions of labor: who ventured into the kitchen to prepare meals, who remained at the table to engage in conversation, who took on the responsibility of clearing the dishes, and who was served first. These actions laid the groundwork for understanding societal expectations regarding masculinity and femininity, often reinforcing stereotypes without overtly acknowledging them.

Emotional economics found its roots in your early experiences as well. You learned that love must be earned through specific behaviors and that silence could be valued more highly than expression. Feelings were often seen as burdens, perceived as inconvenient unless they were smoothed over to maintain another's comfort or happiness. This early conditioning taught you that compliance often came at the expense of your own emotional well-being.

Power dynamics were subtly woven into the fabric of household interactions, where one person's display of anger might be tolerated or even seen as justified. At the same time, assertiveness from another was branded as rebellion. You were groomed to navigate these invisible rules, learning that control is often wrapped in the guise of care and that obedience can be misinterpreted as a form of love. Maturity, in this context, implied the readiness to swallow your own truths in favor of someone else's peace of mind. Your self-worth became inexplicably linked to how much you could give, fix, or absorb without complaint.

These lessons were seldom articulated directly; instead, they were absorbed through sidelong glances, disciplinary actions, household duties, oppressive silences, and sporadic rewards. As these norms became ingrained, you unwittingly became part of a system. A system where self-worth is conditional, thriving in your silence. A system that sanctifies sacrifice as a virtue and sees compliance as a mark of respect. Because this was your entire upbringing, it often masqueraded as love.

Now, even as an adult, the shadows of this system linger. It may not always manifest in the behavior of those around you, but rather in your own actions and reactions. You find yourself shrinking in spaces where you're not even asked to, apologizing instinctively before voicing your thoughts, and second-guessing your need for rest, ease, or the ability to say no. These remnants of your early training still play a silent but powerful role in shaping how you navigate the world, often at the expense of your own authenticity and well-being.

These Archetypes Are Energies We Inherit, Not Identities We Choose

The personas we adopt in our lives are not merely individual choices; they are deeply ingrained elements of an energetic blueprint passed down through generations. Each archetype encapsulates a specific wound or challenge:

Each archetype carries a wound. For example, The Abandoned One holds the deep pain of feeling "I am not important." This can manifest in two ways: as the overachiever who seeks validation through success, or as the invisible one who fades into the background.

- The Overgiver emerges from feelings of guilt, striving to earn love through self-sacrifice. This archetype is frequently identified as the "good spouse," "perfect child," or "ideal friend," forever seeking approval by putting others' needs above their own.

- The Controller is born from chaos and fear, attempting to maintain order through power or perfectionism. This archetype often struggles with the burden of responsibility, trying to create stability in an unstable environment.

- The Outsider feels the sting of rejection due to their perceived differences. This archetype longs for belonging while remaining true to their authentic self, often feeling torn between two worlds.

- The Performer gains recognition for achievements rather than for who they are at their core. This archetype becomes trapped in a cycle of needing to prove their worth constantly to receive love and acceptance.

- The Silent Protector endures quietly, absorbing the emotional pain of those around them without ever voicing their own suffering. This archetype often feels isolated, having never learned to express their own needs and desires.

These archetypes show up in every household, varying only in language and custom, yet rooted in the same underlying energies and inherited fears.

Consider the mother who loses herself in the role of perpetual caregiver, neglecting her own identity in the process. Reflect on the father who, while fulfilling his role as the provider, struggles to nurture emotionally, leaving a gap in affection. Think about the child who carries the emotional weight of the family, often feeling responsible for the happiness of others. Recognize the partner who disappears into their obligations, forgetting their own passions and desires in the name of duty. There's the rebel, often seen as a troublemaker, whose actions cry out for freedom and self-expression. Finally, consider the peacekeeper, who sacrifices authenticity for the sake of approval and harmony.

These expressions are not mere personality traits; they represent energetic imbalances that have been passed down as "normal" within families. The crucial difference lies in how these patterns are treated: in some households, they are hidden away, in others, they are romanticized, sometimes even ritualized, while in others, they are outright denied. Yet, the body and nervous system retain the memories of these experiences, revealing truths that words often fail to express. The energy does not lie; it speaks volumes about what has been endured.

CHAPTER 6: THE MIRROR OF LIFE

EMBRACING RESPONSIBILITY, ENDING ILLUSION

In every journey of awakening, we encounter a pivotal moment, a profound shift that transforms our perspective from merely asking why events unfold in our lives to deeply exploring what these experiences reveal about our true selves. This transition marks the conclusion of one chapter, filled with questions and uncertainty, and the dawning of another, rich with clarity and insight.

As we venture deeper into our inner landscapes, we unearth facets of our identity that have long remained concealed. This transformative process requires us to relinquish deeply ingrained false beliefs and the identities we've constructed for the sake of external validation. We must confront and heal emotional wounds tied to feelings of abandonment, low self-worth, and rejection. Recognition dawns as we uncover the societal masks we donned to navigate life, conforming to imposed roles such as the Good Girl, the Achiever, the Caretaker, the Peacemaker, or the Rebel. While these identities may have garnered acceptance and validation from others, they often overshadow our authentic selves and the profound wisdom that resides within.

In the early stages of awakening, an overwhelming sense of grief can manifest. We grieve the person we once were, the roles we played, the silences we tolerated, and the sacrifices we made in pursuit of acceptance rather than honoring our authentic needs. It is a challenging yet necessary reckoning, as we realize the discrepancy between who we are and who we've pretended to be.

Awakening transcends mere awareness; it is about integration and action. Awareness without courageous action becomes another loop of suffering; we risk remaining ensnared in painful, repetitive patterns. Such stagnation can lead to obsessive rumination over our challenges or a tendency to shift blame onto ourselves or others. Our journey is one of personal empowerment, a conscious choice to embark on a path of self-discovery, healing, and reclaiming our innate power.

At this juncture, the metaphor of the mirror becomes sacred. In viewing "Life as a Sacred Reflection," we learn to interpret our experiences as profound dialogues between our soul and the universe, reframing them as opportunities for growth rather than failures. Each interaction, be it with a partner, a colleague, or a family member, serves as a lesson, shedding light on aspects of ourselves. For instance, if a partner appears emotionally distant, it may highlight our need to cultivate self-love. If a supervisor tends to micromanage, this could reflect our own struggle to trust in our capabilities. Sometimes, our strongest emotional reactions to others, criticism, judgment,and envy are mirrors reflecting aspects of ourselves we've disowned or suppressed. Life invites us to reintegrate these fragments, not with shame, but with compassion and curiosity.

These reflections invite us to investigate our lives without suggesting something fundamentally wrong with us. Instead, they illuminate the areas within ourselves that require healing and consciousness. In reflecting on our past, we may confront moments when life felt unjust or love was perceived as unsafe. Each rejection we faced, reshapes our path, and every struggle equips us with the resilience needed for a more conscious and fulfilling existence.

The challenge lies not in over-analyzing our pain or assigning blame, but in embracing personal accountability. By doing so, we can acknowledge our past experiences without allowing them to dictate our future. We assume ownership of our healing journey, understanding that while we have been influenced by others, we possess the power to choose our responses.

Awakening is not about fixing perceived flaws but rather about rediscovering our authentic selves beneath layers of societal expectation and personal suffering. By embracing life as a mirror, we align ourselves with our true essence, free from the constraints of roles defined by others.

In our quest for alignment, we turn our focus toward reclaiming our inner clarity, wisdom, and agency. We cultivate a posture of gratitude for every experience that has shaped our journey, recognizing that our past, whether deemed a blessing or a burden, acts as a guide leading us toward our authentic truth. Rather than perceiving life as an adversarial struggle, we learn to view it as a reflective surface, inviting us to move forward with heightened awareness and purpose, poised to embody the light that we seek.

The Mirror Of Life

In every journey of awakening, we encounter a pivotal moment,a profound shift that transforms our perspective from merely asking why events unfold in our lives to deeply exploring what these experiences reveal about our true selves. This transition marks the conclusion of one chapter, filled with questions and uncertainty, and the dawning of another, rich with clarity and insight.

As we venture deeper into our inner landscapes, we unearth facets of our identity that have long remained concealed. This transformative process requires us to relinquish deeply ingrained false beliefs and the identities we've constructed for the sake of external validation. We must confront and heal the emotional wounds tied to feelings of abandonment, low self-worth, and rejection. Recognition dawns as we uncover the societal masks we donned to navigate life, conforming to imposed roles such as the Good Girl, the Achiever, the Caretaker, the Peacemaker, or the Rebel. While these identities may have garnered acceptance and validation from others, they often overshadow our authentic selves and the profound wisdom that resides within.

In the early stages of awakening, an overwhelming sense of grief can manifest. We find ourselves mourning the person we once were, grappling with the roles we've inhabited, the silences we've endured, and the sacrifices we've made in pursuit of acceptance rather than honoring our authentic needs. It is a challenging yet necessary reckoning, as we realize the discrepancy between who we are and who we've pretended to be.

Awakening transcends mere awareness; it is about integration and action. If we possess awareness without the courage to act, we risk remaining ensnared in painful, repetitive patterns. Such stagnation can lead to obsessive rumination over our challenges or a tendency to shift blame onto ourselves or others. Our journey is one of personal empowerment, a conscious choice to embark on a path of self-discovery, healing, and reclaiming our innate power.

At this juncture, the metaphor of the mirror becomes sacred. In viewing "Life as a Sacred Reflection," we learn to interpret our experiences as profound dialogues between our soul and the universe, reframing them as opportunities for growth rather than failures. Each interaction, be it with a partner, a colleague, or a family member, serves as a lesson, shedding light on aspects of ourselves. For instance, if a partner appears emotionally distant, it may highlight our need to cultivate self-love. If a supervisor tends to micromanage, this could reflect our own struggle to trust in our capabilities.

These reflections invite us to investigate our lives without suggesting something fundamentally wrong with us. Instead, they illuminate the areas within ourselves that require healing and consciousness. The challenge lies not in over-analyzing our pain or assigning blame, but in embracing personal accountability. By doing so, we can acknowledge our past experiences without allowing them to dictate our future. We assume ownership of our healing journey, understanding that while we have been influenced by others, we possess the power to choose our responses.

In reflecting on our past, we may confront moments when life felt unjust or love was perceived as unsafe. Acknowledging these experiences as integral parts of a larger tapestry reveals their significance and purpose. Each rejection reshapes our path, and every struggle equips us with the resilience needed for a more conscious and fulfilling existence.

Awakening is not about fixing perceived flaws but rather about rediscovering our authentic selves beneath layers of societal expectation and personal suffering. By embracing life as a mirror, we align ourselves with our true essence, free from the constraints of roles defined by others.

In our quest for alignment, we turn our focus towards reclaiming our inner clarity, wisdom, and agency. We cultivate a posture of gratitude for every experience that has shaped our journey, recognizing that our past, whether deemed a blessing or a burden, acts as a guide leading us toward our authentic truth. Rather than perceiving life as an adversarial struggle, we learn to view it as a reflective surface, inviting us to move forward with heightened awareness and purpose, poised to embody the light that we seek.

ΔΔΔ

ALIGNMENT

CHAPTER 7: WHAT IS ALIGNMENT, REALLY?

Alignment is an ongoing journey rather than a fixed goal. It represents the harmony that emerges when your values, beliefs, emotions, thoughts, and actions work together, much like an orchestra playing in perfect sync. Achieving alignment is not about being perfect; it's about finding agreement with yourself and living authentically.

Many people mistakenly equate alignment with consistently being right or having complete control over every aspect of their lives. However, true alignment is flexible and rooted in honesty. It allows for imperfections and encourages growth, inviting you to embrace both your strengths and your vulnerabilities.

When you are aligned, your actions naturally reflect your true beliefs. You become aware of and honor your feelings instead of suppressing them to fit into societal expectations. In this state of alignment, life feels more manageable and effortless; you no longer feel the need to portray false happiness or seek approval from others to validate your worth. Your decisions become guided by a deep inner understanding rather than driven by fear or external pressures, empowering you to respond thoughtfully to challenges.

Before discovering alignment, life can feel like a series of automatic reactions fueled by unresolved pain, inherited beliefs, and unmet needs. Once you begin to align, you cultivate a heightened awareness of your energy and motivations, prompting you to ask important questions about your choices before you act. Aligning with your truth transforms into a daily practice, serving as both your guide and a means to connect with the universe. This process of transformation starts not with dramatic changes but with consistent, small choices that reflect what feels true and respectful to your own identity.

Pillars Of Alignment

Clarity of Inner Truth

Alignment starts with a fundamental skill: knowing what is true for you.

This may seem simple, but for most of us, it's one of the most challenging and most transformative things we can do: unlearning the noise we've been taught and beginning to listen to ourselves genuinely.

From the moment we are born, we are given a script to follow: "Be good. Be quiet. Be helpful. Be successful. Be selfless. Be strong. Be likeable. Be feminine. Be masculine. Be enough."

We adhere to this script so consistently that, by the

time we reach adulthood, most of us struggle to differentiate between the parts of our identity that we chose and those that were imposed on us. The distinction between our conditioned "yes" and our soul's true "yes" becomes blurred. We agree to things that drain us and reject dreams that intimidate us. We label it as maturity, responsibility, or love. However, deep down, we realize that we are betraying something essential within ourselves.

Alignment begins with the courage to pause and ask ourselves: "Is this truly me, or is this what I've been programmed to be?"

Clarity starts not with strategy or intellect, but with the sensation in your body that reflects what is true or false for you. Your "yes" arises from resonance; it feels open, alive, and clear. Conversely, your "no" feels heavy, sticky, and tight. Over time, many of us learn to ignore these signals. We convince ourselves to stay in situations we have outgrown, often saying "yes" out of guilt, fear, or obligation. We forget that every false "yes" is a betrayal of the self, while every brave "no" is an act of alignment.

Clarity is not about knowing everything; it's about understanding yourself in the moment. You don't need to justify your truth with evidence or over-explain your decisions. It's essential to trust that your body knows the difference, even if your mind hasn't yet found the words.

In the early stages of alignment, confusion often masquerades as truth. You may find yourself asking:

- "What if I'm wrong?"

- "What if I'm being too rigid?"

- "What if they'll be hurt if I change?"

However, confusion is often a sign that you're stepping outside your programming. It represents an in-between space where the old self has loosened its grip, but the new self hasn't fully settled in. In this space, you are learning discernment.

Discernment is the ability to sense what is aligned without succumbing to self-doubt. It allows you to differentiate between what is true and what is familiar, between your intuition and your trauma response, and between your values and the values imposed by someone else's pain.

As you develop this skill, you may experience discomfort. That's okay. Clarity doesn't always feel calm at first; sometimes, it manifests as shaky hands and a brave voice declaring, "This isn't for me anymore."

Throughout our lives, we carry narratives and identities that have been passed down to us, often from family, culture, or societal expectations. These stories can shape our self-perception in profound ways. Phrases like:

- "You're the responsible one."

- "You always take care of others."

- "You're the ambitious one."

- "You're the obedient daughter."

- "You're the peacemaker."

- "You're the one who never complains."

These roles, while they may have brought us recognition, safety, and a sense of belonging, can also confine us, hindering our authentic selves. They create a rigid framework that may not align with who we truly are or with our deepest aspirations.

To move toward a life of true alignment, it's essential to examine the roles we've adopted and question their relevance in our lives today. Just because a particular identity assisted in our survival, providing comfort and stability within our family dynamics, does not necessarily mean it continues to serve our growth or aligns with our purpose. The roles we once embraced might now feel like chains, binding us to outdated versions of ourselves.

Letting go of these inherited identities can evoke a sense of grief. You may find yourself mourning the loss of the approval that came with these roles or grappling with uncertainty about your identity without them. This transition, however, can lead to profound liberation, a realization that you were never meant to perform a part in someone else's script. Ultimately, you were meant to embody a complete, multifaceted person.

One of the most significant shifts we can make on our journey toward alignment is learning to listen to our intuition rather than succumbing to the programming of societal norms and expectations. For years, we may have followed the voice of "should," dictated by fear, external pressure, or even internalized shame. This voice often leads us down paths that don't resonate with our true selves, causing disconnection and distress.

In contrast, embracing alignment empowers us to rediscover and honor the voice of truth within us. This voice is softer yet infinitely stronger, a quiet whisper that encourages authenticity. It might say:

- “You’re allowed to want what you truly desire.”

- “You’re not too much; you are ready to step into your fullness.”

- “You don’t have to make yourself small to maintain harmony.”

- “You were never broken; you were merely buried under layers of expectations.”

Intuition speaks not through loud proclamations but through gentle nudges, an energy, a sensation, or a subtle knowing that resides just beneath the surface of our consciousness. To access this wisdom, we must cultivate practices of stillness, such as deep breathing, mindfulness, and active listening. By allowing ourselves to slow down, we create space for our intuition to rise, guiding us toward choices that honor our authentic selves.

As you begin to live in alignment with this intuitive voice, the world around you may appear to shift, not because external circumstances have changed, but because you have chosen to stop abandoning yourself to fit preconceived molds. Embracing your true self opens new possibilities, relationships, and experiences that resonate with your core being, allowing you to thrive rather than merely survive.

Living from Your Truth is Powerful

When you start to honor your true self, you may upset those who are still holding on to their own beliefs. You will stop acting in ways that make others feel comfortable. You will make choices that others may not understand. You may lose their approval, but you will gain something more valuable: your true self.

Living true to yourself isn't about finding the perfect path in life. It's about following the inner guidance that leads you there.

The more you return to your truth by making each choice in line with it, the more freedom you will feel. As you become freer, you also inspire others to do the same.

Understanding Nervous System Regulation

Before we discuss intuition and energy, we need to talk about the body and the nervous system. This system shapes how we experience and interpret our feelings.

Most of what we call intuition or "gut feeling" comes from the state of our nervous system. If your body is on high alert, tense, overwhelmed, and flooded with stress hormones, then even your best instincts may feel unclear. You might think you're being bold, but you could just be reacting out of fear. You might call it surrender, but it could actually be freezing up. You might think you are being selfless, but it could be people-pleasing. We can't connect with truth if we don't regulate our nervous system; we just end up repeating past traumas in new situations.

To live in alignment, your body needs to feel safe.

Why Regulation Matters

The body keeps memories that the mind might forget. Unpredictable childhood experiences, unsafe environments, conditional love, pressure to please, and punishment for expressing yourself all become part of your body's memory. You might grow up, become a parent, or take on a new role, but your body can still tense up at loud voices or conflict. It still interprets feedback as rejection. This isn't your fault, but it is your responsibility.

Nervous system regulation is not just a wellness trend; it's part of your personal growth. It's the missing link between knowing what you want and being able to accept it. It bridges healing with living fully.

What Is Regulation?

Nervous system regulation means bringing your body back to a natural state of safety and awareness. It allows you to feel without becoming overwhelmed. You can pause without shutting down and breathe without bracing yourself. Regulation isn't about staying calm all the time; it's about returning to balance when needed.

Calmness is a skill, not an inherent trait or privilege.

Many people are out of sync and don't realize it. They think they are just overthinkers, procrastinators, or angry people. The truth is, they are scared. Their nervous system is trying to protect them from an unnamed threat. Until they rebuild this sense of safety, genuine alignment feels out of reach.

The Trauma Responses: Fight, Flight, Freeze, Fawn

When you feel unsafe, your body instinctively reacts in one of four ways:

- Fight: You argue, control, or confront. Anger serves as protection.

- Flight: You escape or avoid. Staying busy covers up your fears.

- Freeze: You feel numb, shut down, or stuck. It's like being in a fog.

- Fawn: You go out of your way to please others. Keeping peace becomes a survival tactic.

These responses are not flaws; they are coping mechanisms that once kept you safe. Recognising them is the first step. Appreciate them, then decide to shift your behaviour.

Practices to Rebuild Safety

You cannot think your way to regulation; you must feel your way there. This is the start of true engagement.

- Breathwork: Deep breathing sends safety signals to your brain. Try long exhales, like 4-8 breaths or box breathing, to help you center yourself.

- Grounding: Walk barefoot on the ground. Feel your feet. Press your palms against a wall. Bring yourself back to the present.

- Cold Exposure: A quick splash of cold water or a brief cold shower can help reset your stress response and increase your tolerance for discomfort.

- Somatic Tracking: Pause to ask yourself, "Where do I feel this in my body?" Breathe into that area, and give it attention. This builds trust in yourself.

- Shaking or Movement: Allow your body to move naturally. Let yourself tremble, dance, or shake off tension when you feel activated.

These practices are about being present, not about performing. Just a few minutes each day, done regularly, will teach your body that it is safe to feel, to pause, and not to hide. In this safety, alignment can blossom.

Each time you choose breath over panic, movement over shutdown, and honesty over people-pleasing, you are rewiring your nervous system. You are building resilience, which is essential for real alignment to develop.

Nervous System as a Spiritual Practice

Regulation is more than just healing; it is a way of maintaining mental clarity. It helps you separate fear from intuition. It teaches you to remain open, even when memories demand that you protect yourself. Without this work, we can inadvertently repeat old patterns instead of embracing new opportunities.

CHAPTER 8: BELIEF REPROGRAMMING

A DEEP DIVE INTO YOUR EMOTIONAL ARCHITECTURE

Beliefs shape not just our thoughts but also the emotional framework within which we perceive and interact with the world around us. They serve as the foundational blueprint from which our experiences and realities emerge. Surprisingly, many of these beliefs are not consciously chosen; instead, they are inherited, absorbed, and embedded within our subconscious through various channels such as childhood experiences, cultural conditioning, generational wounds, and repeated emotional patterns throughout our lives.

To align with the life your soul genuinely aspires to experience, it is essential to dismantle and re-evaluate the old beliefs that were likely instilled in moments of fear, confusion, or survival. This reprogramming isn't about deceiving yourself with false narratives or masking your feelings with toxic positivity. Instead, it involves confronting the root of these beliefs with honesty, clarity, and conscious choice. This journey is not about erasing your past; it's about reclaiming the authentic self that has been overshadowed by scripts that were never truly yours.

Identifying Subconscious Beliefs

The first step in this profound journey involves cultivating awareness around the beliefs that quietly dictate your daily life. These beliefs often manifest in thoughts such as:

- "I must work harder to earn my worth."

- "I feel like I don't belong anywhere."

- "If I express my true thoughts, I'll be abandoned."

- "There will never be enough resources for me."

- "Success is only achievable through struggle."

- "I have to be perfect to be deserving of love."

Such beliefs are not mere fleeting thoughts; they reside deep within the nervous system and influence how you respond to opportunities, relationships, and challenges that arise. If your body instinctively recoils at the thought of receiving love, money, rest, or visibility, a hidden belief is likely obstructing your alignment with abundance.

These subconscious beliefs often arise from three significant sources of emotional pain:

1. Scarcity: A sense of lacking in love, safety, time, financial resources, or validation.

2. Worthlessness: The feeling of being insufficient, invisible, or easily replaceable.

3. Fear of Rejection or Abandonment: The belief that love is conditional and can be easily lost.

To transform your external reality, it is imperative to access and shift these deep-seated inner codes.

Tools for Belief Reprogramming

Effective belief reprogramming is not about forcefully adopting new beliefs but rather about rewiring your emotional body and forging new neural and energetic pathways that feel safe, authentic, and expansive.

1. Inner Child Healing

Many of your subconscious beliefs were formed during childhood, often before the age of seven, during times when cognitive reasoning was limited. Your emotional self internalized meaning from experiences that felt unsafe, confusing, or overwhelming. Inner child work is about reconnecting with these earlier versions of yourself, not to fix them but to hear and validate their needs, pain, and experiences. Reflect on questions like:

- "What did I need to hear as a child that I never really heard?"

- "What beliefs did I internalize based on actions not taken or words unspoken?"

- "Which part of me still carries that unmet need for love and safety?"

This process is not about changing into someone else; it's about embracing your wholeness by welcoming back all the disowned parts of your being.

2. Subconscious Journaling

Instead of approaching journaling logically, allow yourself to write from a deeper, more instinctual place. Start with prompts that help you dive into your emotional landscape:

- "I fear that if I let go of control, then..."

- "The belief I hold about being seen is..."

- "The first time I felt unsafe in love was..."

Let your inner world spill onto the page without censorship and then examine it closely: Whose voice is this you're hearing? Is it yours or an echo of something absorbed from others?

Awareness is paramount to the reprogramming process.

3. Affirmations and Visualization (Done Effectively)

Affirmations should not be mindlessly repeated if they evoke feelings of resistance or disbelief within you. Instead, they should gently guide your system towards a truth you are ready to accept. Use bridge statements, such as:

- "I am learning to trust in myself."

- "I am gradually opening to the concept of safety in love."

- "More and more, I am choosing to believe in my intrinsic worth."

Couple affirmations with vivid visualization: imagine scenarios where the believed truths come to life for you. Engage all your senses in the process. How would it feel to navigate life, trusting in your own voice? To allow yourself to rest without guilt? Or to receive financial abundance simply for being your true self? The body does not differentiate between imagined and lived experiences; it internalizes what is emotionally repeated.

Ultimately, true alignment involves selecting beliefs that are rooted not in fear, shame, or trauma, but in the authentic knowing of your soul. Some transformative shifts might look like:

- From "I must earn love" to "I am inherently lovable."

- From "Life is a continual struggle" to "Life flows abundantly when I am aligned."

- From "I need to do everything alone" to "I am supported by both seen and unseen forces."

- From "I must prove my worth through achievements" to "My very presence is enough."

You don't need to fully believe these new truths right away. Start with a willingness to entertain the possibility of their existence. Allow the energy of potential to permeate your being.

Reprogramming is a continuous journey, not a one-time task. It requires daily devotion. It calls for a conscious return to your truth, a practice of recognizing the lies you've internalized, pausing, and gently choosing anew.

Remember, you are not striving to "fix" yourself; you are engaged in a journey of removing what was never yours, making space for your soul to guide you towards a more authentic existence.

Energy Hygiene & Boundaries

As you work to reprogram your subconscious beliefs, you will develop a heightened sensitivity, not a sign of weakness, but a clear understanding of your needs. This clarity will help you identify what drains your energy, what nourishes it, and what no longer aligns with your truth. However, awareness is just the first step; to truly align with your higher self, you must establish energetic containment. This is where energy hygiene and boundaries become essential.

You cannot step into a soul-led life while leaking your energy into the needs, emotions, expectations, or chaos of others. You cannot embody your higher self if you remain entangled in guilt, obligation, or invisible contracts from your past. Every belief you reprogram requires a boundary to contain its new frequency.

Leaky Energy vs. Contained Energy

Leaky energy manifests as a constant feeling of being "on", emotionally responsible for others, overthinking your image, struggling to say no, or acting out of obligation instead of genuine choice. You may find yourself absorbing others' moods, adjusting your truth, or getting pulled into situations that leave you drained or resentful.

This energy dynamic is familiar among those conditioned to please others, who are hyper-tuned to others' emotions, or who grew up without modelled or respected boundaries. It transcends mere "niceness"; it comes from survival patterns ingrained to secure love or safety.

In contrast, contained energy signifies true energetic sovereignty. You are acutely aware of your energetic field. You understand where you end and others begin. You take full responsibility for your thoughts, feelings, and actions, releasing the burden of carrying what isn't yours.

This doesn't equate to indifference; it means stopping the energy leaks. You will no longer pour emotional energy into dynamics lacking respect, reciprocity, or resonance.

To reclaim contained energy, ask yourself:

- Am I acting from alignment or fear?

- Am I over-explaining due to feeling unsafe in saying no?

- Do I feel free in this space, or do I feel trapped, obligated, or guilty?

Remember, boundaries aren't walls. They are doors you consciously choose to open or close based on discernment.

Saying No Without Guilt

The challenge many face isn't simply saying no; it's navigating the imagined emotional fallout, guilt, confrontation, and fears of being perceived as selfish, rude, or ungrateful. However, guilt is not always a marker of wrongdoing; more often, it signals that you're breaking a generational or emotional pattern.

When you choose your energy, time, and needs, especially in dynamics built upon self-abandonment, discomfort will arise. This discomfort is merely the echo of your old identity fading away. You need to learn to sit with this discomfort.

Saying no without guilt is a skill and a practice. It is a spiritual boundary that declares, “I refuse to betray myself to uphold illusions of harmony.” You do not owe anyone access to your inner world just because they have been accustomed to it. Relationships rooted in love will evolve alongside your truth. In contrast, those anchored in control, guilt, or unconscious need will resist your growth.

Let them resist. Your aligned life cannot rest on unaligned agreements.

Detaching from Guilt, Obligation, and Control

A significant portion of our energy is tied up in silent contracts: “I will be who you want me to be to avoid rejection.” “I will keep giving so you won’t leave.” “I will remain silent to keep the peace.” These contracts are often subtle, and you may not realize you’ve agreed to them. Yet your body knows. The signs, fatigue, a tight chest, and resentment signal energetic bondage.

Guilt, obligation, and control stem from fear: fear of being unloved, excluded, misunderstood, or branded as "too much." However, true alignment cannot coexist with these energies.

To break free from them:

- Forgive yourself for who you were before you understood that you have a choice.

- Reclaim your right to revise agreements that no longer reflect your current self.

- Honor the discomfort, recognizing it as evidence that you are prioritizing your soul over conditioning.

Detachment does not imply indifference. It means trusting others with their journeys while remaining devoted to your own.

Healthy Energetic Separateness (Especially in Families and Partnerships)

This work is crucial and is often most tested in close relationships. In families and partnerships, there tends to be a deep sense of enmeshment: “I feel bad if you feel bad.” “I’ll diminish myself to keep you comfortable.” “Let me manage your emotions so I can feel needed.”

True love does not require such enmeshment. It honors individuality, allows space, and respects boundaries without misinterpreting them as abandonment.

Energetic separateness means:

- You are not your partner’s emotional regulator.

- You are not your parent’s caretaker.

- You are not your child's saviour.

- You are not your family's unpaid therapist.

You can love deeply while still maintaining your boundaries. You can stay connected without losing your individuality.

CHAPTER 9: ALIGNED ACTION

EMBRACING THE PATH OF AUTHENTIC LIVING

Alignment isn't fully realized until it manifests through our actions. You might possess a deep understanding of your truth, foster a strong sense of power, and express your boundaries with clarity; however, until your actions mirror your authentic self, the transformation remains largely internal. Embodied alignment is what bridges the gap between inner work and outward expression, allowing for a life that resonates with your true essence.

Contrary to the frenetic pace that society often celebrates, aligned action emerges not from urgency, the desire for approval, or the fear of missing opportunities. It is not simply about cramming your calendar with activities or ticking off milestones to validate your worth. Instead, aligned action is a slow, sacred, and sovereign process that honors your unique journey.

When you find yourself in a state of dysregulation, feeling ungrounded or disconnected from your core values, your actions can become chaotic and reactive. In these moments, it's easy to acquiesce to external demands, saying "yes" when your intuition urges you to decline. You might act out of avoidance, fleeing from the stillness that holds the potential for insight. In contrast, aligned action is clean and purposeful. It arises from a grounded inner "yes," characterized by a sense of right timing and profound inner resonance. There's no confusion; approval is unnecessary, and, crucially, aligned action leaves you energized rather than drained or resentful.

Before hastily attempting to fix, change, or plan your next steps, alignment calls for a period of being. It prompts you to sit with discomfort, to create space for inquiry, and to truly listen to your inner voice. This tranquil space of "being" is the fertile ground where clarity is born. From this stillness, new ideas, insights, and choices can emerge organically. Thus, when you take action from this place of presence, it becomes magnetic, effective, and imbued with peace.

Many individuals wait for a dramatic moment to catalyze change, whether that's quitting a job, launching a business, or ending a relationship. However, alignment doesn't thrive on drama; it is grounded in precision. Often, the tiniest shifts can lead to significant transformations, like updating your phone wallpaper to reflect your vision, choosing not to respond immediately to a triggering message, or adjusting the tone of your voice when interacting with a child. Alignment begins with micro changes that gradually build into macro impact. Those who master this understanding recognize that meaningful change is often quiet, consistent, and intentional.

Impulse can often masquerade as urgency. You might experience a surge of energy, face a fear, or respond to an external cue, leading you to act hastily. Conversely, inspired action has a distinct quality. It typically follows a period of rest or reflection, bubbling up from a place of internal clarity, not from panic, but from purpose. You might sense a compelling inner pull, an idea that resonates deeply, or a conviction that "now is the time." At this juncture, action transforms into something powerful, creative, and in harmony with your soul's journey.

Perhaps the most profound expression of aligned action is knowing when to hold back. The ability to pause, to refrain from responding, and to resist the impulse to "do something" just to alleviate discomfort is, in itself, alignment. In relationships, business situations, or parenting, there are moments when waiting becomes the wisest course of action. Cultivating this inner awareness enables you to discern when to leap with confidence and when to hold steady. This deep listening is a vital resource that alignment fosters.

Each aligned action serves as an anchor and a declaration of who you are becoming. You move not out of fear, performance, guilt, or external expectations but from a place of truth. When your actions begin to reflect your internal shifts, transformative change in your external world follows suit. Embracing this journey of aligned action allows for a life that feels authentically yours, resonating with a deep sense of purpose and intention.

CHAPTER 10: EMOTIONAL AND ENERGETIC ALIGNMENT

True alignment in our lives calls for more than a superficial understanding of our emotions; it demands a profound sense of emotional responsibility. This means embracing our feelings fully, with compassion and understanding, without shifting blame onto others or external circumstances. Until we learn to take ownership of our emotional landscape, we remain vulnerable to the whims of other people's behavior, unpredictable events, and the unresolved scars of our past. Emotional responsibility demands that we acknowledge our feelings without suppressing or controlling them. It's essential to honor their existence, yet we must not use them as weapons or let them define who we are.

One of the most transformative milestones on the path to emotional maturity is recognizing the distinction between simply experiencing an emotion and projecting it onto someone else. Often, we find ourselves caught in a cycle of unconscious projection, lashing out, withdrawing, straying into criticism, guilt-tripping others, or shutting down entirely. Yet, these responses don't stem from the actions of others being "wrong." Instead, they arise from the turmoil within us that remains unprocessed and unacknowledged.

To process an emotion is to create a safe space for it. It involves naming it, breathing into it, and allowing it to flow through us. Whether it's through journaling, taking long walks, crying, or even shouting into the privacy of a pillow, processing encourages us to engage with our emotions as our personal journey. It's an act of acknowledgment where we disentangle our feelings from the people around us. By becoming aware of what triggers us, we reclaim our inner space, moving towards clarity and understanding.

In contrast, projection acts as a defense mechanism. When we project, we deflect our emotions outward, often causing rifts in our relationships. Processing, however, is a sacred return to self, a reaffirmation of our autonomy in the emotional realm.

As we delve deeper into our emotional experiences, it is crucial to understand that we are not defined by our feelings. We are the ones who experience emotions, and there exists a significant difference between saying, "I feel sad," and declaring, "I am sad." The former allows for the experience of sadness as a passing emotion, while the latter confines us to a fixed state of being. Similarly, "anger is moving through me" should never become synonymous with "I'm an angry person."

When we over-identify with our emotions, they begin to morph into personality traits, rigid narratives that color our perceptions of the world around us. True alignment invites us to feel fully without succumbing to the weight of emotional collapse. Emotions serve as messengers, not masters of our lives. We can cry without feeling broken and channel our rage without inflicting harm. The key lies in observing our emotions, honoring their presence, and allowing them to flow without building a rigid identity around them.

Like clouds drifting through the sky, emotions are transient. They shift and pass when we refrain from clinging to them or judging ourselves for their existence. In a state of alignment, we acknowledge that each wave of emotion carries invaluable insight, yet no singular emotion defines our worth, essence, or truth.

Among the emotional burdens we carry, shame, guilt, and resentment are some of the heaviest, often borne silently for years. Shame whispers that we are inherently wrong, while guilt insists that we have done something wrong. Resentment, a particularly insidious feeling,arises when we suppress our truths in favor of others.

These emotions are frequently inherited, culturally reinforced, and conditioned into our psyche. Shame is often rooted in familial dynamics, where expressing our needs led to feelings of punishment or inadequacy. Guilt surfaces when we start honoring ourselves in environments that previously demanded our self-sacrifice. Resentment festers when we continually abandon our own needs to preserve harmony, seek approval, or avoid conflict.

Healing these burdens commences with awareness and a commitment to honest expression. It requires us to speak what often remains unspoken, unravelling the narratives that have long held us captive. We must learn to forgive ourselves for the versions of ourselves that existed before we knew better, to release what was never ours to bear.

These emotions are signals indicating that our boundaries have been crossed, that something within us needs to be expressed or integrated, and they are not meant to persist indefinitely. Aligned individuals do not shy away from shame or guilt; instead, they navigate through these feelings with gentleness, embracing the truths they reveal.

Emotions function as our internal compass, intricately woven into the fabric of our beings. Each sensation we encounter holds a message, a call to either align with our true selves or to steer away from it. Feelings of joy, peace, and expansion signal that we are moving closer to our core truth, while sensations of contraction, dread, or exhaustion alert us to areas of our lives that are out of sync.

When we listen closely, our emotions illuminate the path to our deepest truths. That unsettling pit in our stomach when we agree to something that doesn't resonate. The tightness in our chest around certain individuals. The warmth and openness in our hearts when we speak from the soul. The exhilaration that surges through us when we pursue our innermost desires.

In a state of alignment, emotions are not problems to be solved; rather, they are messages to be trusted. They guide us toward healing, unveil hidden truths, and reveal the love waiting for us on the other side of discomfort. We grow into a state of emotional sovereignty, empowered to feel deeply while responding wisely, no longer subject to the sway of every comment, rejection, or mistake.

In embracing this journey of emotional responsibility, we not only enrich our lives but also cultivate more meaningful connections with others, creating a ripple effect of understanding, compassion, and authentic living.

Reflections:

Clarity blooms from inner stillness and spaciousness. Your truth is always present, sometimes hidden beneath noise, fear, or conditioning. Engage in these transformative practices to uncover it:

Morning pages / Freewriting

Each morning, pour your thoughts onto paper without hesitation. Allow your unconscious to express itself. Over time, your truth will emerge from the depths of your habitual mind.

Body-Based Check-Ins

Inquire within: "Where in my body do I feel this?" Place your hand there. Emotions reside in the body. A choice that feels heavy or contracted may signal misalignment, while lightness and calmness often indicate alignment with your truth.

Silent Walks In Nature

Let nature liberate you from mental clutter. Without distractions, simply walk and ask: "What's true for me right now?" Listen intently to the answers that surface in the stillness.

- Meditative inquiry
- Pose profound questions such as:
- "What am I avoiding?"
- "What do I truly desire if no one else had an opinion?"
- "What does my inner child need to feel safe?"

Sit quietly with these queries in meditation, allowing answers to arise from deep within, unclouded by logic.

Voice recording / Soul dialogue

Articulate your feelings aloud as if conversing with your soul. Hearing your own voice reveal raw emotions bypasses mental filters and uncovers deep truths.

The mind conveys habitual thoughts; the soul resonates with true desires. Discerning the difference involves a journey of deconditioning.

Here's how:

Track the origin of the thought

Ask: “Where did I learn this?”

If a belief or desire feels rigid, fear-driven, or tied to seeking approval, take a moment to pause. Was this influence inherited from family, culture, religion, or education?

True desires radiate expansiveness, even when unfamiliar. Conditioned beliefs often bring shame, pressure, or urgency.

Test the ‘If nobody knew’ filter

Reflect: “Would I still want this if no one saw or praised it?”

This question unveils the authenticity of your desires. True desires remain steadfast, even without external recognition.

Notice your energy

Conditioned beliefs feel heavy, obligatory, and tense, shadowed by mental chatter. True desires exude calmness, steadiness, and a gentle yet persistent light.

Recognize fear vs resonance

Fear whispers: “What if I fail? What will others think?”

Resonance, however, speaks: “This feels like me. I want to explore it.”

Resonant desires echo a soft ‘yes’ in the heart, even if they defy logic.

3. What steps can I take to embrace discomfort while developing discernment in my alignment journey?

Discomfort marks the path of realignment and signifies growth. Cultivating the ability to navigate this discomfort fosters discernment. Embrace these steps:

Befriend discomfort (Somatic presence)

When discomfort arises, pause. Instead of fleeing, inquire: “Where is this in my body?” “Can I breathe into it without the need to fix?” The body harbors unprocessed emotions; clarity unfolds when you remain present with discomfort.

Choose discomfort that leads to truth, not comfort that maintains lies

Familiar patterns (pleasing, avoiding conflict, overexplaining) may feel cozy, but they aren't necessarily aligned.

Reflect: “Am I opting for peace or merely evading a storm?” Embrace the fleeting discomfort of truth over the enduring weight of dishonesty.

Sit in the pause before reacting

In conversations, decisions, or triggering moments, pause. Create a space between stimulus and response. It is here that discernment flourishes.

Track your patterns

- Maintain a journal of instances when:

- You acted out of guilt.
- You agreed when you truly meant no.
- You shied away from confronting a difficult truth.

Over time, these patterns will reveal themselves, guiding you toward more mindful responses.

Reclaim Your Desire and Joy

Desire is not a weakness; it's sacred. It is the pulse of life, the whisper of your soul urging you to engage deeply with the world around you.

For too many of us, desire has been skewed by societal norms and personal experiences into something to be feared or suppressed. We've been conditioned to believe that wanting too much makes us greedy, selfish, or unworthy of happiness. Over time, joy has morphed from our natural state into a luxury we feel we must earn, and pleasure has become a transaction requiring permission from ourselves or others.

This is where we lost our way:

We stopped listening to the whispers of our inner compass, the longings, the exhilarating moments of excitement, the soul's inner spark that declares, "This is for me." We learned to stifle that spark in favor of being "practical," "selfless," or "responsible." A life devoid of authentic desire becomes mechanical. It loses its vibrancy and essence, robbing us of the colorful tapestry of experiences we crave.

To reclaim your joy is to grant yourself permission to want deeply and unashamedly. This is not a matter of ego, but rather an act of honoring your very essence. Reflect on the following questions without guilt or self-judgment:

✧ What do I truly want to feel, create, experience, and express? Consider the diverse aspects of your life, your passions, dreams, and the quiet yearnings that stir within you.

✧ What brings lightness to my body, even when the weight of the world feels heavy? How can you nurture these moments of liberation and joy amidst life's challenges?

✧ Where did I learn to associate softness with weakness? When and how did society teach us that pleasure could be a distraction? Why have we made joy an obligation that requires justification?

Often, the answers to these inquiries lead us back to early conditioning, maybe it was in childhood, when self-sacrifice was celebrated, and our personal needs felt burdensome to those we loved. Perhaps it was in a culture that ridiculed the pursuit of pleasure, instilling guilt in those who dared to seek joy.

Unlearning these patterns isn't synonymous with indulgence; it is about reclaiming wholeness and authenticity in a world that often demands conformity.

Desire is the innate language of your soul,a guiding force that gently steers you toward experiences that are expansive and nourishing. And joy? Joy is the profound state of being you rediscover when you transition from mere survival to truly living. It is in the moments of authenticity that you find your wildest dreams beginning to align with your reality.

Let joy be your medicine, the salve for your soul's wounds.

Let desire be your compass, guiding you through the intricate maze of life.

Let pleasure be your teacher, not as an external performance, but as a vibrant force that resides within you, illuminating the path to fulfilment.

Reclaiming your desire means courageously moving toward what feels deeply authentic and fulfilling, even if your passions are small or misunderstood by others. It's about embracing your softness and sensuality, standing firmly in your right to a life that is not merely functional, but rich and fulfilling.

Your joy is not trivial.

It is your unique frequency, resonating through the universe.

It is your power, the force that infuses life with meaning.

It is your unequivocal "yes", a declaration of your existence and your right to experience everything life has to offer.

Dive into those desires; let them lead you toward a life where joy is not a distant dream but a daily reality. Reclaim your desires, and you will find a deeper connection to yourself and to the world around you. The journey is yours, and every step toward your joy is a step toward reclaiming your truth.

Integrity in Relationships

You cannot have alignment and performance at the same time.

A major realization happens when a person understands that many of their relationships are not based on mutual honesty, but on unspoken agreements. These agreements can look like this:

- Love is exchanged for compliance.

- Closeness is maintained through emotional effort.

- People value your presence for what you do instead of who you are.

These patterns may not be clear at first; they can seem like love. Here are some examples:

- A daughter adjusts her behavior to fit her parents' emotions.

- A partner downplays her own wishes to keep the peace.

- A friend listens continually but doesn't feel safe to share openly.

- A woman feels guilty for saying no, even when she is tired.

These patterns can look supportive, but they come with an invisible cost: you lose parts of yourself to keep the relationship stable.

Dismantling the Performance Identity

One tough truth about spiritual alignment is this: you cannot be true to yourself and perform at the same time.

Integrity means being honest, and also being true to what you feel, believe, need, and how you act. Performance is bending your truth to fit in, avoid conflict, or keep an outdated identity.

Many people don't realize they are performing. They think they are being helpful or mature. But, if you look closely, what seems like "kindness" may be appeasement, "strength" may be suppression, and "compassion" may arise from a fear of being alone.

Spiritual growth prompts you to stop and be honest with yourself, not to blame others, but to stop betraying yourself.

Many people choose to stay silent. Speaking truth can feel risky, especially when you have held the same roles in relationships for years. You might disrupt familiar patterns, disappoint others, or stop being seen as the easy or nice one.

But here is an important point: if your truth disturbs the connection, the problem is not with your truth; it is with the relationship's structure. Relationships built on hidden expectations fear clarity, while those built on integrity require it.

Speaking your truth doesn't always mean you must confront someone. Sometimes it means you stop pretending. It might involve stepping back or changing your tone or availability. It always requires you to listen to your inner voice.

The Collapse of the Pleaser Archetype

People often misunderstand pleasing others as generosity. In truth, it can be a form of neglecting yourself. This pattern starts when love and safety become mixed up with approval.

When people praise you for being “sweet,” “thoughtful,” or “accommodating,” you may start to think your worth comes from helping others, not from who you are. Over time, this belief becomes a burden. You may grow tired of always anticipating others' needs and stop paying attention to your own. Your soul may ache because no one, not even you, asks what you truly need.

The turning point occurs when you realize that real connection does not require sacrifice; it requires owning your own needs. Sometimes, the most honest love means disappointing others to meet your own needs.

Love vs. Loyalty: A Difficult Differentiation

In families, friendships, and partnerships, loyalty can seem sacred. However, you need to examine the loyalty you feel.

Are you loyal to the person, or to a pattern? Are you committed to love, or to obligation? Many people stay in mismatched relationships because they fear being seen as disloyal. But there is often quiet suffering when we betray ourselves for the sake of duty.

Loyalty can become harmful when it involves emotional manipulation,when guilt is used to keep you from being yourself or when you must sacrifice to prove your worth. You may start to feel trapped in love rather than free within it.

Love should not require you to give up yourself to stay connected. Alignment should not require suppression in exchange for peace. As you grow, your relationships must also evolve. Not all relationships can grow with you, and this can be a grief but also a liberation.

Many dysfunctional relationships arise not from a lack of love but from unexamined roles we play. Roles like the fixer, nurturer, over-functioner, silent one, or peacekeeper often start in childhood and repeat in adulthood.

While these roles may make you feel secure or functional, they can also keep you hidden. When you relate to others through these roles, the true you gets filtered through the expectations placed on you.

CHAPTER 11: LIVING FROM SOUL, NOT EGO

Living in alignment means learning to listen to your soul's quiet truth instead of letting the ego run your life. The ego isn't something we need to fight; it's just a set of old patterns, shaped by fear, comparison, and survival instincts. But to stay aligned, we must notice when we've shifted from presence to protection.

Catching Ego in Everyday Life

You'll often find the ego show up in small, sneaky ways:

- You over-explain yourself in a conversation, just to be understood.
- You say yes when you want to say no, afraid someone might feel bad.
- You feel tense because a plan didn't go as expected, and you're silently blaming yourself or someone else.

These are ego reactions: control, fear, and the need for validation. In alignment, you begin to catch yourself in these moments, not with shame, but with awareness. You pause and ask: *Is this my truth? Or am I trying to protect an old version of me?*

Making Space for the Soul

Living from the soul is a soft, grounded choice. It means you don't rush to fix discomfort; you sit with it. You don't chase validation, you check in with your own resonance. You stop managing how others see you and start focusing on how you *feel* when you're alone with yourself.

This shift doesn't require perfection, it requires presence. Simple daily practices help:

- When you feel triggered, take three deep breaths before responding.
- When your mind spirals, place a hand on your heart and ask: *What part of me needs love right now?*
- Instead of reacting in an argument, say: *Let me take a moment to return to clarity.*

These moments create space between ego and soul. And in that space, your truth can emerge.

Ego Deaths and Rebirths

Spiritual alignment will challenge the old roles and identities you've outgrown. You may stop being the fixer in your family, the achiever in your work, the peacemaker in every argument. And that can feel like a loss. But it's also a return to who you were before the world told you who to be.

For example:

- You once believed success meant being busy all the

time. Now, rest feels more powerful.

- You thought being "a good daughter" meant saying yes to everything. Now, your no is spoken with love and self-trust.
- You used to panic when someone misunderstood you. Now, you let it go, because your truth doesn't need defending.

These are ego deaths, when the old you crumbles so something more honest can be born. You may feel raw and uncertain in these transitions. But you'll also feel lighter. Because every layer you shed brings you closer to your essence.

Alignment isn't a fixed state; it's a relationship you build with yourself over time. It asks for honesty, surrender, and a willingness to walk into the unknown with your heart open. The more you choose soul over ego, the more you feel a deeper calm, one that doesn't depend on what's happening around you.

This chapter of your life isn't about proving anything. It's about becoming fully yourself. And in that becoming, you naturally inspire others, not through effort, but through embodiment.

Daily Practices and Lifestyles of Alignment

Stillness, Silence, and Spaciousness

In a fast-paced world that seems to spin quicker each day, we find our senses bombarded by endless notifications, looming deadlines, and an unrelenting drive to achieve more. True silence and genuine stillness have become almost rare, even intimidating. Yet, it is within these infrequent pauses that profound alignment starts to take shape. This doesn't happen because we've finally checked off every task, perfected our routines, or proved our worth; rather, it occurs when we embrace the quiet and spaciousness, allowing ourselves to reconnect with who we truly are.

In today's culture, busyness is often equated with success. The thought of pausing, of allowing time to stretch without the pressure of productivity, can make us feel anxious, restless, or fidgety. From a young age, we've been taught to fill every available moment, measuring our days by checklists and accomplishments. We often feel that if we're not doing something, we're either missing out or falling behind.

But what if those in-between spaces are where the magic truly happens? Picture waking up one morning and choosing not to reach for your phone immediately. Instead, you sit quietly with yourself, savoring your first sip of coffee by the window, watching the sky shift its hues. At first, your mind may buzz with all the tasks that await you. Yet, if you simply breathe, taking in the warmth of the mug, the soft sounds of nature, and the gentle rhythm of your breath, a shift begins to occur. In this space, you open yourself to insights and guidance that are often obscured by the noise of striving.

Finding peace in nothingness is a courageous act. Many of us, influenced by culture and habit, go to great lengths to avoid it. Those moments that seem empty, when nothing is resolved or clear, can feel frightening or meaningless. Yet, deep down, our souls crave these pauses. Think of them as fertile soil, calm on the surface yet rich in possibility beneath.

It is in these in-between moments, between jobs, relationships, breaths, that we find ourselves gradually realigned. Instead of pushing for a quick resolution, greet these moments like an old friend. With a sense of patience and curiosity, ask yourself: What new growth could be stirring in this pause?

White space is often seen as wasted time, but it is, in fact, a refuge for your inner life. It's the conscious choice not to fill every moment, allowing your mind and body to relax and noticing what rises when there's no pressure to perform.

White space can take many forms:

- Allowing emails to sit unanswered, even when your mind clamors for closure.

- Enjoying a peaceful walk without headphones, simply attuning to the whispers of your own thoughts.

- Holding off on diving into your digital world in favor of ten minutes of quiet, gently settling into your body and breathing.

- Intentionally carving out pauses, brief breaks between meetings, moments to close your eyes and listen within, spaces to let your nervous system breathe.

Far from being empty, these moments can overflow with insight. In the quiet, creativity awakens, intuition sharpens, and your core values come to light. You might be surprised by the subtle shifts that occur, the gentle nudges or flashes of inspiration that rarely break through when your mind is cluttered.

Stillness isn't an act; it's a way of being. It invites a deeper kind of listening, one that perceives more than just words or thoughts. In stillness, you begin to notice bodily sensations, the flow of energy, and emotional currents that usually go unnoticed in the hustle of daily life.

You might catch yourself reaching for your phone out of habit, scrolling without purpose, or reacting impulsively to someone's words. In those moments, pause and gently ask yourself, "What is my heart genuinely seeking right now?" The immediate urge may be for relief or distraction, but underneath, you may uncover a deeper longing for connection, peace, or clarity.

Stillness gives you the opportunity to observe triggers without acting on them. After a difficult conversation or conflict, allow yourself to linger in silence, feeling the discomfort without rushing to explain or defend. Listen for what lies beneath, the softer truths that harsh words or quick reactions often hide.

When your mind is constantly buzzing, the wisdom of your soul becomes mere background noise. Lowering this volume, creating intentional moments for silence, is how true presence comes to light. In presence, alignment unfolds effortlessly, blossoming quietly and without fuss. The deepest wisdom, clarity, and renewal arise not from noise or hustle, but from the quiet richness of simply being here, now.

Let stillness be your trusted ally. Welcome the spaciousness that may feel foreign at first, allowing it to reveal what you truly need. Trust that the most significant changes in your life start in the open, unhurried silence, the white space where you can rediscover yourself. In these gentle pauses, you will find not emptiness, but a wealth of understanding that patiently awaits to guide you forward.

Routines That Regulate and Realign

While alignment is fundamentally an inner state of being, it requires the support of outer structures that nurture our nervous system, promote mental clarity, and foster spiritual openness. Routines should not be viewed as mere rigid frameworks or benchmarks of perfection; rather, they represent the rhythm of our daily lives. These routines remind us to engage with our true selves repeatedly, especially in a world that often attempts to pull us outward and distract us from our core.

Morning Rituals: Grounding & Intention Setting

The way we start our day significantly shapes the energy and mood that follow. The first few moments after waking act as a threshold. How we step into that threshold dictates whether we embark on our day with centered clarity or succumb to the chaos of scattered thoughts and distractions.

A grounding morning ritual doesn't need to be elaborate; it can be elegantly simple yet profoundly effective. Consider incorporating practices such as:

Mindful Breathing: Spend three minutes sitting in silence, focusing solely on your breath before you reach for your phone. This practice centers your mind and settles any racing thoughts.

Heart-Centered Inquiry: Place a hand on your heart and ask yourself, "What do I need today?" This moment of introspection helps in clarifying your intentions and aligning with your inner truth.

Intention Crafting: Write down a singular, clear intention for your day. Phrases like “I choose peace today” or “I allow flow and joy” can serve as powerful anchors.

Gentle Movement: Engage in gentle physical activity such as stretching, yoga, or taking a short walk. This not only wakes up your body but also helps you ground yourself in the physical world.

These morning rituals serve to reorient your focus from external pressures to your internal reality. They create a sacred space for you to define the energy you wish to embody as you navigate the demands of the day.

Night Rituals: Release & Integration

Evenings present an opportunity for reflection and closure. They gently prompt us to release the burdens we’ve carried throughout the day and to integrate the experiences and lessons we’ve encountered. Without a conscious ritual at day’s end, we risk dragging the energetic remnants of stress, unresolved conversations, or mental clutter into our sleep.

A night ritual can function as a profound emotional exhale. Consider including elements such as:

Journaling: Dedicate time to note what you are letting go

of from the day be it stress, self-doubt, or the projections of others. This practice helps clarify your thoughts and emotions.

Body Awareness: Perform a body scan before sleep, consciously noticing any areas of tension and inviting relaxation into those spaces.

- Closing Mantra: Speak a closing affirmation such as, “I did enough. I am enough. I release the rest.” This creates a mental ritual of acceptance and completion.

- Calming Tools: Utilise soothing elements such as warm herbal tea, aromatherapy, or soft music. These sensory experiences can calm your nervous system and signal to your body that it is time to rest.

When your body understands that it is safe to rest, your energy has the opportunity to reset more profoundly, enabling you to awaken refreshed and renewed.

Body-Mind-Soul Check-Ins

Throughout our busy days, alignment may occasionally

waver, and that's completely natural. The more essential aspect lies in how swiftly we recognize and return to our centered state.

Check-ins are mindful pauses that invite us to reconnect with ourselves. They may unfold as questions such as:

- Physical Needs: "What does my body need right now? Do I require rest, hydration, or movement?" Tuning in can prevent burnout and enhance well-being.

- Thought Patterns: "What's the tone of my thoughts? Am I spiraling in fear or aligned with possibility?" This awareness helps redirect our mindset towards positivity.

- Authenticity of Action: "Does this action feel pressured, or does it resonate as true?" Recognizing the difference can prevent us from acting out of obligation instead of desire.

- Emotional Boundaries: "Am I inadvertently holding someone else's emotions as my own?" This reflection encourages emotional intelligence and self-care.

By committing to regular check-ins, whether before accepting an invitation, sending a message, or powering through exhaustion you start honoring your personal rhythm. Over time, these micro-moments of reconnection cultivate a life that feels grounded, authentic, and deeply fulfilling.

Aligned Environments

Have you ever paused to consider how much our surroundings influence our energy? The truth is, environments are far from neutral; they either uplift us or drag us down, shaping our present while echoing the past. On the path to alignment, awareness of our external spaces becomes just as crucial as exploring our inner selves.

Your Home, Digital Realm, and Connections

Think of your home as more than just four walls; it's an emotional and energetic sanctuary. When clutter piles up, or when we neglect certain corners, they can harbor stagnant energy, keeping us trapped in old emotional patterns. The same holds true for our digital environments: what we consume online, the people we follow, and the content filling our screens subtly influence our subconscious.

And let's not forget our relationships each interaction, whether a quick message or a deep conversation, serves as either a reflection of our alignment or a signal of where we might have veered off track.

Reflect and Ask:

- Does this space radiate clarity or chaos?

- Do these conversations empower me or limit me?

- Is my digital life fostering growth or holding me back?

Alignment invites us to be intentional curators not for the sake of perfection but for genuine energetic integrity.

Revitalise Your Spaces: Energetic Detox

Just like our bodies require rest and a detox, our environments need intentional clearing to thrive. This goes beyond mere cleaning; it's about maintaining energetic hygiene.

Here are some ways to refresh your spaces:

- Light some incense to cleanse stagnant energy.

- Open windows regularly to invite fresh air and light.

- Play uplifting music or chants to elevate the emotional ambiance.

- Let go of items that feel heavy or tethered to a past self.

- Evaluate your digital feeds and unfollow accounts that skew your self-image.

Remember, energetic detox isn't just spiritual, it's essential psychological maintenance. By releasing what no longer resonates, we create a welcoming space for alignment to flourish.

Crafting Spaces That Embody Your Future Self

The most vibrant environments don't just look good; they are visionary, they embody the person you're evolving into.

Here's how to create spaces that inspire:

- Curate objects, books, art, and colours infused with intention.

- Design your layout to promote flow, peace, and creativity.

- Write down affirmations or vision statements and place

them in high-visibility spots.

- Surround yourself with reminders of what truly matters: beauty, depth, freedom, and integrity.

Your outer space is like a personal mirror. When it reflects your alignment, you create a safe haven to be your truest self. If it doesn't, your body will inevitably react and notice the tension, irritation, or numbness. Pay attention.

Alignment isn't just a whisper of clarity inside you, it's the vibrant courage to unleash your truth into the world. Self-expression acts as a bold bridge, connecting your inner wisdom with how you present yourself on the outside. Without it, alignment can feel like a private ritual, silently simmering away. But the moment you dare to speak, move, create, or dress in harmony with your true self, you transform mere knowledge into living, breathing authenticity.

How often do we hold back out of fear, fear of being misunderstood, overlooked, or judged? We tighten our words and clip our wings before we even attempt to soar. But remember: your voice is meant for expression, not editing. Speaking up isn't about being the loudest; it's about being genuine. Even the softest whisper can resonate like gold when it comes from a place of presence and authenticity.

Your voice matters in every form it takes: the boundary you establish, the poem you dare to craft, the story you choose to share. Each time you express your truth, you reaffirm your trust in your own journey.

- Speak your desires boldly, without shrinking them for others.

- Voice your fears bravely, without shame or apology.

- Share your messy, luminous journey not for validation, but to free your soul.

Exploring Art, Words, Style, and Movement

Self-expression isn't confined to spoken words. It bursts forth in the way you move, the outfits you choose, the music that envelops your day, and the art or laughter you create. It lives in every dance move you make when no one is watching, in every vulnerable line you dare to write, and in the energy you radiate in any space.

Imagine what you would wear if judgment didn't exist.

What would you paint, sing, or create if joy were your only measure of success?

How would your body move if self-consciousness weren't a factor?

These questions open the door to pure freedom. Authenticity isn't about perfection; it's about being true to yourself and the world around you. It's allowing your emotions and energy to flow, leaving your unique imprint wherever you go.

Creating Without the Weight of Judgment

Judgment, whether from others or ourselves, can stifle

creativity, pulling us away from our true center and into a hollow performance. Alignment compels you to create simply to breathe easier and feel fully alive.

You don't need to be an acclaimed artist, a celebrated poet, or a social media star. Authentic expression is about showing up as your raw, real self, illuminating the world with your glorious colors unfiltered and beautifully imperfect.

Cook with love? That's art.

Dress with intention? That's true style as truth.

Write with honesty? That's alignment, ink flowing onto the page.

Make authentic expression a daily practice for your soul. It's a path back to yourself, not a performance for the applause of others. When you step into expression without fear, you burst forth from shame and embrace freedom. You become a mirror for others; your courage lights the way. And before you know it, your life becomes your loudest, most beautiful voice.

CHAPTER 12: RESISTANCE & SETBACKS ON THE PATH OF ALIGNMENT

Even on a soul-aligned path, resistance doesn't simply disappear; in fact, it may become more intense. As you begin living in alignment, your old beliefs, such as struggle, self-sacrifice, and the need for control, start to feel out of place with the person you are becoming. However, your nervous system might not be fully on board yet.

Initially, you may question this discomfort, wondering, "Why am I feeling off when I'm doing everything 'right'?" This is a common moment when many people retreat, not because they aren't ready, but because the feeling of expansion can feel unfamiliar and unsettling.

Often, the real fear isn't about failing; it's about what could happen if you actually succeed. Thriving requires adopting a new emotional reality, one where you are seen, loved, supported, and flowing with ease. While this may sound beautiful, for someone who has learned to associate safety with struggle, it can feel very threatening.

You might hesitate, not because your path is wrong, but simply because it feels new.

When your soul begins to expand, your ego goes into panic mode. It whispers doubts: What if this doesn’t last? What if you lose yourself? What if you alienate others? Unconsciously, you may start to stifle what wants to grow.

This is where things often become tricky. Life starts to feel good aligned, even magical, but something inside you doesn’t trust it. You may find yourself second-guessing your joy, overthinking decisions, replaying old conversations, or creating drama where there was none. This behavior isn’t because you seek suffering, but rather because a part of you, conditioned to chaos, doesn’t yet know how to embrace peace.

Self-sabotage isn't a sign of being broken; it's a protective mechanism. Your body and mind respond to the gap between your new reality and your old programming. You may not fully believe you deserve to feel this good without facing repercussions.

As a result, instead of moving forward, you might stall, retreat, or create conflict to regain a sense of "normalcy."

But this is where alignment becomes powerful not because it eliminates sabotage, but because it equips you with tools to recognize it in real time.

Walking in alignment doesn't mean you stop being

human; you will still experience triggers and doubts. However, how you respond starts to change. You learn to notice when old fears arise, not with judgment, but with curiosity. You can ask yourself, "Is this my aligned self speaking, or my fearful self?"

Instead of spiraling, you ground yourself. Instead of reacting impulsively, you pause. Instead of trying to fix others, you focus on caring for yourself.

This shift isn't about achieving perfection; it's about being present. It's about choosing to stay with yourself through discomfort and reminding your body, "We're safe now. We're not living in the past anymore."

Each time you interrupt an old pattern with a new response, you expand your ability to stay aligned.

As your capacity to navigate resistance deepens, you may find yourself experiencing a heightened spiritual sensitivity. This heightened awareness extends beyond just an understanding of your emotions; it opens you up to a more profound connection with energy, the subtle nuances of timing, synchronicities that seem to guide your path, and those intuitive nudges that call for your attention. Your inner landscape transforms into a richer, quieter, and remarkably vibrant space, filled with insights and revelations.

However, this increased awareness can present a new set of challenges most notably, the challenge of staying grounded amidst the exhilarating waves of spiritual growth. As you align more closely with your authentic self, you might receive an influx of insights, creative downloads, vivid dreams, and an overarching sense of higher guidance. While these experiences can be empowering and illuminating, they also risk pulling you away from your earthly existence if not approached mindfully.

This is where the concept of spiritual bypassing can subtly intrude. You may find solace in using affirmations or positive thinking to mask deeper emotions when what you truly need is to process your grief or confront the turmoil within fully. Phrases like “everything happens for a reason” can serve as a coping mechanism while you bypass the raw, unresolved ache that resides in your chest. When positivity is wielded as a shield against discomfort, it transforms into a form of escape rather than a means of genuine integration.

True alignment is not synonymous with unceasing happiness; rather, it embodies the idea of wholeness. Wholeness embraces every facet of the human experience, including sadness, anger, fear, and the inherent messiness of life. It also acknowledges the presence of doubt and contradiction, which are natural parts of our journey. If you strive to bypass the heaviness of your emotions by only reaching for the light, you risk creating a spiritual schism, one that disconnects you from the richness of your human experience.

To stay grounded in your spiritual journey, it is crucial to avoid the temptation to escape into lofty ideals or heavenly aspirations before you have anchored yourself firmly to the earth. This involves returning to your body and reconnecting with the basic elements of everyday life. Engaging in practices that ground you, such as mindful breathing, nature walks, or simply allowing yourself to feel and express your emotions, are essential steps in this transformative journey. Only through this rootedness can you fully embrace your spiritual evolution while honoring the entirety of your human experience.

EMBODIMENT

CHAPTER 13: WHAT IS EMBODIMENT?

Embodiment isn't about putting on a show. It isn't a checklist of affirmations to recite or a game of sounding spiritual. It doesn't lie in the clever Instagram captions, the fancy retreats, the self-help books you've devoured, or the knowledge you've stored in your mind. No, the embodiment is quiet and subtle. It reveals itself in the way you breathe in private, in how you respond when life throws you curveballs, and in the choices you make each moment not to impress others, but because those choices resonate deeply within your very being.

To embody something means to weave it into the fabric of your life, not just in your mind, but in your body, emotions, and energy. When you truly integrate what you believe, it transforms into how you live. The truths you once scribbled on paper manifest in your nervous system, your tone of voice, your boundaries, the way you walk into a room, and how you approach conflict with clarity and softness rather than fear or control.

True embodiment requires no validation. It

communicates through your energy rather than words. There's a presence about you an alignment that others pick up on even before you utter a single word. That's the kind of truth your body remembers. Energy doesn't lie. You might curate a polished image, but your frequency will always resonate louder. You can project perfection, but if your actions are tinged with resentment, fear, or shame, people will sense that, too. Embodiment means there's no divide between what you value and the reality you create. Your beliefs, movements, and essence are all unified.

This is why I often say we're not merely here to tally up the pain, trauma, or wisdom we've gathered; we're here to become the living embodiment of those experiences. We're not out to prove we're healing; we are the evidence of what's possible when healing becomes part of our identity. It shifts us from merely surviving to truly living, from clenching for control to finding coherence, from performing knowledge to embodying wisdom.

And let me be clear: embodiment is not a rush job. It humbles you and demands time, repetition, and integrity. It doesn't reward how quickly you grasp something; instead, it roots you in how completely you become it. Often, the most embodied individuals aren't the loudest voices in the room. They create safety without needing to explain themselves. They move with intention, speak only when it counts, and rest without guilt. They don't push or persuade, they attract, inspire, and transmit.

Your body isn't just a vessel; it's the living archive of your journey. It remembers what your mind might forget, holding wisdom that transcends words. This is why genuine change can't happen solely through mindset shifts. You can read all the right things and still live in fear. You might understand boundaries conceptually yet fail to embody them in relationships. You might meditate daily and still find yourself spiraling into shame or reactivity when faced with triggers. Unless these insights land in your body, they remain mere concepts.

Embodiment is that landing. It's the process of returning to yourself so often that the truth becomes your home not just an idea, but a tangible reality. As a result, you begin to show up differently. You stop leaking energy seeking approval or understanding. You stop giving away your power for fleeting peace. You stop trying to fix others and start witnessing them. You drop the act of performing healing and start living in wholeness.

You become the transformation you've been yearning to create.

This is what authentic activism looks like, not loud demands but quiet alignment. Not just preaching change, but becoming the essence of the future. Your embodied presence creates ripples and opens a field of permission. There's no need to convince anyone to grow; your very existence serves as the invitation. And that's the power of embodiment, it doesn't just shift your personal narrative; it transforms everything your energy encounters.

So, the real question isn't how much you know. It's about how much of that knowledge you're living. How does your body uphold truth when under pressure? How does your nervous system react to discomfort? Are you responding from alignment or falling into reaction? Do you lead from a place of peace or from performance? Ultimately, embodiment isn't about how others perceive you; it's about whether your soul feels at home in your body.

And when it does? That's when the world starts to feel your presence differently.

The journey from knowing something to truly living it can be subtle but deeply impactful. After we explore ourselves through reflecting on our past, writing in journals, or participating in rituals, we reach a point where we need more than just information. We seek a sense of alignment. This is what it means to embody our knowledge.

At this important moment, our questions change. Instead of asking, "What else do I need to learn?" we start asking, "Am I living out what I already know?" This is when wisdom becomes a part of us, a place where our insights can guide us.

As we go through this process, we may feel a mix of emotions. Many people find comfort in being self-aware, using it as a shield against vulnerability. Identifying a problem can feel like a way to control it if I understand why I struggle, maybe I can avoid the pain. However, embodying our knowledge requires us to be more honest. It asks us to move beyond mere performance and be genuinely present.

We might reach a stage where sharing our stories of past struggles feels heavy, like carrying an unnecessary load. This isn't denial; it's a choice to let go. Realizing that we often hold onto our past identities, including our coping strategies and survival behaviors, can prevent us from living in line with our true selves.

Letting go of these old identities doesn't mean we have to fight them. Instead, we choose not to support them anymore. When we stop nurturing the parts of ourselves that sought worth through busyness or used kindness to control others, we can develop a more authentic self. This isn't about abandoning our spirituality it's about being honest with ourselves.

By accepting this challenging yet beautiful change, we open up space for true self-expression.

Becoming more aware of your body and feelings takes practice. Here are some simple ways to help you with this process:

1. Body-Based Grounding: Try activities like breathing exercises, cold showers, or walking barefoot outside. These can help you feel more secure and present.

2. Micro-Honesty: Practice being truthful in small ways each day. Say no when you mean it, hold back laughter when someone says something wrong, and express your true thoughts without adjusting them for others.

3. Daily Body Check-Ins: Pause and ask yourself, "What does my body need right now?" instead of asking, "What should I be doing?"

4. Silence and Solitude: Spend time alone to focus on feelings you haven't processed yet, like grief, gratitude, anger, and clarity.

5. Living Your Truth: Show your true self in small, everyday actions. Choose to rest instead of distracting yourself, create space instead of trying to make everyone happy, and seek alignment over approval from others.

These steps are not about significant changes; they are simple ways to change your daily life with awareness.

Navigating the Discomfort of Identity Shift

Changing from who you were to who you really are can be tough. It often feels messy and confusing. Your body might see this change as unsafe, even if it helps you make better choices.

To manage discomfort without going back to old habits:

- Name Without Judgment: Notice your feelings without criticizing yourself. Recognize when you feel scared or when you try to control things; this helps you process emotions without being overwhelmed.

-Create Transitional Rituals: Use music, movement, warm baths, or time in nature. These rituals help you feel safe during changes.

- Rehearse Safety: Speak kindly to your scared self. Remind yourself, "You are safe now. I'm not leaving you; we are just doing things differently."

- Find Community or Solitude: Pay attention to what your body needs. Too much outside stimulus can confuse you, while too much alone time can make you feel uneasy. Listen to your body's needs.

Remember, feeling uncomfortable doesn't mean you are off track; it means you are growing beyond your limits.

Setting boundaries may feel like building walls at first: scary, stiff, and protective. But as you grow, boundaries can turn into flexible agreements based on what feels right, not on rejection.

To bring boundaries into your life

- Start with Energetic Boundaries: Practice saying no by simply not participating. Your absence can send a message without drama.

- Align Boundaries with Values: Make your boundaries reflect your values, not guilt. For example, say, "I want to be around people who uplift me," instead of "I can't come because I feel drained."

- Listen to Your Body: Notice how different interactions affect your energy. Use this information to shape your boundaries.

- Allow Boundaries to Evolve: Understand that a firm 'no' today can shift to a 'maybe' tomorrow. Your boundaries change as you do.

- Practice Grace Over Justification: When your boundaries become part of who you are, you won't need to explain them as often. Your presence will naturally communicate them without conflict.

Over time, boundaries become less about what you say

and more about what you allow. You will clearly see what you no longer accept.

This journey, moving from knowledge to real change, doesn't need outside approval. Inside, everything shifts; you become less reactive and more open. You move away from controlling behaviors and start living consciously.

In this new space, you no longer change your truth for others. You stop seeking your worth from outside sources. Instead, you show the power of being true to yourself, living authentically and embodying who you are.

You don't get to embody your truth in isolation. Embodiment shows up in the messiness of relationships. In how you love. In who you choose. In what you tolerate. In how you show up even when your wounds want to run. It's one thing to speak about boundaries and sovereignty; it's another to hold them when you're in love, afraid, or grieving.

This is the real work: staying in your body when it's easier to abandon yourself for the high of someone else's attention, speaking your truth even when it risks losing the connection. Walking away from someone who feels familiar, but not safe. That's where embodiment lives, not in what you say, but in what you choose when it costs you comfort.

So many people fall in love, or rather fall into a version of love that's confused with longing, fantasy, and unresolved need. They attach to people who feel familiar, not because there's alignment, but because the chaos feels like home. And then they wonder why love feels exhausting, why it hurts, why it comes with anxiety, obsession, and confusion.

Here's the truth most aren't told: you don't attract what you deserve, you attract what your nervous system believes is familiar. And until you regulate that, until you come home to your body, you will confuse intensity with intimacy. You will keep calling in people who push you to prove, perform, or lose parts of yourself just to stay connected.

Embodiment is what breaks this cycle. It's what teaches you to *feel* your way through instead of *fix* your way through. To stay rooted in your body when attraction floods your system. To slow down when your patterns want to rush. To notice when your heart is open but your body is bracing. This is where discernment lives in the body, not in the fantasy.

You must train yourself to notice: "Do I feel safe with them or am I just addicted to the rollercoaster of being seen and unseen?" You must ask: "Do I trust their energy or am I just filling a gap in myself?" These questions matter, because until you get honest with yourself, you will keep making choices that betray your inner truth in the name of love.

Real, embodied love doesn't feel like adrenaline. It feels like breath. It doesn't confuse you. It grounds you. It doesn't ask you to shrink, prove, or earn. It asks you to *be*. And that means the journey begins with you. You have to stop asking, "Why do they do this to me?" and start asking, "Why do I keep choosing this?" Not from shame, but from awakening.

To embody love, you have to start *being* what you say you desire. You want safety? Be safe for yourself. You want consistency? Hold consistent boundaries. You want presence? Learn to stay with yourself when old wounds get loud. That's how you stop confusing drama for depth. That's how you stop abandoning yourself when love gets uncomfortable.

Heartbreak, then, becomes something else. It's no longer proof that love failed, it's proof that your body remembered what it needed. The pain is real, but the clarity it brings is sacred. When you start listening to your pain, not just running from it, you begin to ask better questions. You begin to feel the cost of your old patterns. And you start to honor yourself more deeply.

This doesn't mean you won't feel longing. Or grief. Or the ache of release. It means you meet those emotions without betraying yourself to escape them. It means you don't run back to someone just because you're afraid to sit in the silence. You allow the discomfort to reshape you, to purify your field. And in doing that, you become someone who no longer settles for the half-hearted, the chaotic, the almost.

People often ask, "How do I stop attaching to the wrong ones?" The answer isn't in policing your feelings, it's in getting honest about your needs. When you neglect your own emotional and energetic nourishment, you chase crumbs from others. When you don't know how to hold yourself through emptiness, you'll grab onto whoever fills the space. But when you begin to tend to your body, your emotions, your inner child you become more discerning. You don't attach out of lack. You connect from fullness.

Embodiment teaches you that not every connection needs to be kept. Not every attraction is sacred. Just because someone triggers something deep in you doesn't mean they're meant to stay. Some people come to reflect your wounds. Others to awaken your standards. Few will meet you where you truly are. But that's okay because the more you embody your truth, the less you need from others to feel whole.

Let go of the fantasy that love will save you. Love won't do the work for you. But when you start doing the work, you'll notice the quality of love you attract begins to shift. It becomes cleaner, calmer, clearer. You no longer play games to feel desired. You no longer abandon your voice to feel worthy. You embody it all: your voice, your value, your vulnerability.

This is what it means to be in an embodied relationship. You're not looking for someone to complete you. You're looking to *expand* with someone who reflects your wholeness. Someone who speaks your nervous system's language of peace. Someone you don't have to chase or control because both of you know how to meet yourselves first.

Embodied love isn't perfect, but it's present. It's not always easy, but it's clean. It requires you to stay. To speak. To soften. To walk away when it costs your alignment. And to open again, not from hope but from wholeness.

That's the path. It's not a concept. It's a practice. And the more you live it, the less you'll question it because your body will know: this is love, and this time, I'm not abandoning myself to feel it.

CHAPTER 14: THE WORLD THROUGH AN EMBODIED LENS

When you begin to embody your truth, something radical happens: you stop waiting for the world to change. You stop outsourcing responsibility to the government, to your partner, to your boss, to society. You begin living as though you are the shift because you are.

This isn't a lofty idea; it's a lived reality. The way you wake up, the way you prepare your food, the way you speak to someone in a moment of frustration… these are not just habits. These are declarations. You are constantly announcing your values to the world. Every gesture, every silence, every yes or no, it all speaks.

Being the change doesn't mean becoming perfect. It means becoming congruent. There's no point preaching love if your own heart is filled with resentment. There's no wisdom in tweeting about rest while shaming yourself for taking a nap. The world you want to live in must first live inside you. Otherwise, it remains an idea, not a frequency.

You don't need to start a revolution. You are one. The food you consume, the companies you support, the voices you amplify, the friends you nourish, the language you speak, it's all activism. It's all part of your living, breathing politics.

But this is not the kind of politics that divides. This is the politics of presence. Of coherence. Of saying: *I will not wait for permission to live in alignment.* You stop begging institutions for recognition, and instead begin weaving your values into how you shop, rest, work, create, and connect. You embody your truth rather than argue about it. You become the mirror, not the megaphone.

That's how systems begin to shift not just on paper, but in the very rhythm of your life. You notice yourself detaching from hustle culture, not because someone told you to rest, but because your body no longer tolerates force. You don't glamorize productivity. You respect your own seasons. You move cyclically, not linearly. Some days are in full bloom. Others, deep winter. And it's all sacred.

Your nervous system becomes your compass. If your body contracts every morning at the thought of work, something's misaligned. Embodiment doesn't mean you quit everything; it means you stop abandoning yourself in the name of survival. You stop bowing to urgency. You remember that nature never rushes, yet everything gets done.

That's why embodiment becomes a quiet rebellion. You no longer chase external gold stars, you become your own source of credibility. You hold yourself with deep reverence, even when no one's watching. And when you hold yourself like that, systems begin to dissolve internally first, then externally.

You also start to examine your inner coloniser. The part of you that says, "I must earn rest." The voice that compares, competes, grasps, and suppresses. You name it. You disarm it. You stop letting internalized systems of hierarchy, shame, and guilt dictate your behavior. And over time, your relationships shift. Your home shifts. Your language, decisions, and pace all shift.

This is not about rejecting ambition. It's about rooting ambition in authenticity. Not productivity for the sake of status, but for the sake of service. Not "doing more," but *becoming more honest.* Alignment becomes your structure. Your values become your timekeepers. The body becomes your calendar. Energy becomes your currency.

You stop measuring your worth by what you produce, and begin measuring it by how deeply you live. The joy is in the living, not the proof. There's no competition when you're creating from coherence. There's no rush when you're living in rhythm.

This is what it means to view the world through an embodied lens. You're no longer a participant in unconscious systems, you're a conscious co-creator of something new.

Embodiment and Culture

Where Who You Are Meets the Systems That Shaped You

Embodiment transcends mere introspection. It manifests in how you express your innermost self in environments still steeped in fear, performance, control, and power dynamics. It's about standing in your own truth when the cultural landscape demands conformity.

Let's delve into what this really looks like, not as abstract theory, but as a tangible experience in your daily life, your family dynamics, your relationships, and within your own body.

This journey isn't about aggressive confrontation or trying to out-shout your surroundings. It's about remaining deeply rooted in your own energy, a firm, calm presence that remains unshaken amidst the turbulence around you.

You don't have to mirror the power structures you seek to transform. You needn't adopt aggressive postures or harsh tones to make your voice heard. True power is quiet and steady; it is deeply embodied.

Embracing soft power means possessing a profound understanding of who you are without needing to broadcast it to the world. It involves entering a room and maintaining your authentic self without contorting to fit into others' comfort zones. Your essence speaks volumes, allowing your clarity to resonate instead of feeling the need to defend your position.

You begin to stop explaining your uniqueness. You cease apologizing for your truth. You let go of the compulsion to please in order to belong. Instead, you simply show up soft, strong, and sovereign in your presence.

Initially, this path may feel unsettling. Especially if societal teachings have conditioned you to believe that silence is synonymous with safety or that compliance equates to harmony. However, the more you reconnect with your body and its wisdom, the clearer it becomes: you were never meant to simply blend in. You are destined to shift the atmosphere just by the way you carry yourself.

- I will not perform to gain acceptance.

- I will not shrink myself to receive love.

- I will not harden to command respect.

You transition from merely reacting to actively radiating your essence. That, dear reader, is where the transformation occurs.

For many of us, this topic strikes a deeply personal chord. We often grow up understanding love in contexts that feel perilous, emotionally volatile, unpredictable, or excessively controlling. In the quest for acceptance and belonging, we shape-shift into various roles: the compliant good girl, the silent observer, the perpetual helper, the fixer, or even the rebellious problem child. Each of these roles served as a shield, protecting us amid chaos. Yet, in the process, we sacrificed our authentic selves and the truth of who we are.

You find the courage to no longer abandon your own needs and desires for the sake of inclusion or acceptance.

You recognize that keeping the peace at the expense of your own emotional and physical well-being is a pattern that no longer serves you. Its now that you have seen the pattern and broken it. You choose to stop pretending to be okay for the sake of avoiding conflict, acknowledging that such compromises only breed resentment. You start looking out for yourself.

Instead, you pause to inquire: What feels genuine in my body at this moment? You breathe deeply, anchor yourself in the present, and allow discomfort to flow through you without reacting from a place of fear or unease. You embrace the possibility of being misunderstood by others if it means staying true to your essence.

In this journey, you cultivate your own sense of safety through your breath, your posture, and the tone of your voice, regardless of how those around you may respond. This path does not suggest that you remain in toxic situations; rather, it empowers you to stop performing merely to survive them. By breaking the cycle from within, you reclaim your authenticity.

Many cultures, particularly those built on collective values, are steeped in narratives centered around sacrifice, struggle, and suffering. In this environment, joy is frequently dismissed as naïveté, playfulness is considered frivolous, and a sense of ease is often met with skepticism. Society pushes you to earn your moments of rest, to validate your self-worth, and to prove your love through hardship. If you aren't facing struggles, the insinuation is that you must not be doing enough.

But what if you dared to choose joy despite these constraints? What if you allowed yourself to laugh wholeheartedly, to savor meals at a leisurely pace, to rest deeply not because everything in your life is perfect, but rather because you are finally letting go of the self-imposed punishment? Choosing joy in a world addicted to pain becomes a radical act of defiance.

This declaration asserts:

- I will no longer align my life with guilt and obligation.

- I do not need to endure suffering to demonstrate that I care.

- I reject the notion that stress is synonymous with success.

In making this choice, you shift your connections from pain-based bonding to a place of presence and authenticity. You let joy not merely be a reward for endurance but an intrinsic part of your life philosophy. This doesn't mean turning a blind eye to darkness; rather, it signifies a conscious decision to dwell there no longer. You recognize the presence of grief while simultaneously creating space for joy and light. You honor the pain, but you do not elevate it above the beauty that also exists in your life.

This is the transformative power of embodied joy it can heal without coercion. It uplifts you without necessitating an escape from reality, proclaiming that even within this flawed world, beauty is a choice you can actively make.

Many of us hold a deep desire for our families to heal and evolve. We long for them to cultivate understanding, openness, and emotional growth. Yet, the sobering truth is this: you cannot force anyone to change. Awareness cannot be imposed, nor can you drag someone into alignment with your own values.

What you can do, however, is embody the very qualities and love that you wished had been modeled to you during your upbringing. You stand as a testament to the love that was absent, you speak the truth that your family has struggled to articulate, and you consciously choose to break the cycles they have failed to acknowledge.

Importantly, you do this not to impart a lesson but rather because you have grown beyond the confines of old patterns. You are no longer in a position where you need to convince your parents to respect your boundaries, nor do you feel compelled to prove your worth to your partner or family. You recognize that their healing is not a prerequisite for your own freedom.

Instead, you choose to live out your healing journey fearlessly and unapologetically. Sometimes, your embodiment of truth will inspire others silently; at other times, it might challenge or threaten them. Regardless of their reactions, your responsibility remains unchanged: to persist in living your truth, even in the face of their fears.

Let your groundedness disrupt their controlling tendencies. Allow your calm presence to highlight their urgency. Permit your joy to challenge their ingrained guilt. Let the self-trust you cultivate stand in stark contrast to the shame they attempted to instill in you.

This is how culture transforms from the inside out, not by preaching or trying to fix others, but by simply being.

Challenges and Edge Work in Embodiment

To live as your true self in environments that don't support that truth, whether in a manipulative relationship, a rigid workplace, or a family steeped in guilt and control, requires a kind of quiet courage that doesn't always look loud or obvious. It begins by choosing not to abandon yourself, even when others misunderstand you. You stop overexplaining. You stop performing. You stop begging for understanding from those who are committed to not seeing you clearly. And you do this not from spite, but from a profound clarity that your body, your truth, your peace is no longer up for debate.

This often requires grieving, grieving the version of you who tolerated mistreatment, who stayed quiet to keep others comfortable, who made herself smaller in the name of survival, suffering not only the pain of the past, but the people who can't walk with you into becoming friends who don't resonate anymore. These lovers only loved the version of you that needed them, family who refused to evolve. Embodiment doesn't ask you to cut people off for drama. It asks you to grow so honestly that anyone misaligned will naturally fall away without you needing to force a thing.

And that's where discomfort arises, not just situationally,

but physically. You might feel it as heat in your chest when you speak your truth, or a knot in your stomach when you're about to set a boundary. Your throat might close up when you finally say "no" without guilt. This is not a weakness. This is your nervous system re-learning safety in a new way of being. Let it feel hard. Let it feel unfamiliar. That's the body shedding layers it was never meant to hold.

The mind will want to understand everything, to predict outcomes, to control the narrative. But in embodiment, the body leads first. It knows when something is off before the mind can rationalize it. It senses alignment even when you're scared. The mind may say, "Stay, they didn't mean harm," but the body will whisper, "This is draining you." And over time, as you stop overriding your body's wisdom, it will become easier to trust your inner signals without needing external validation.

This is what the edge looks like: loving yourself enough to stop proving, defending, fixing. Being present with your fear without collapsing. Saying, "This doesn't feel like love," and walking away. Feeling lonely but choosing truth over familiarity. Letting your old self die, again and again, because the version of you you're stepping into can't be carried by the past.

This isn't a weekend retreat. It's a daily practice of choosing your alignment over your attachments. Let it be slow. Let it be real. Let it be messy. Because when your truth becomes your foundation, even in hostile terrain, no one, not even your former self, can take it from you.

CHAPTER 15: WHO DO I CHOOSE TO BE, AND WHAT ENERGY DO I EMBODY IN THIS WORLD?

This is where archetypes come alive, not as labels or costumes to wear, but as timeless, universal energies that live within us all. These are the patterns that exist beyond our personal stories. They are ancient, encoded, primal. And yet, they are deeply relevant to our present moment.

We're not speaking about archetypes as abstract ideas or characters to mimic. This isn't mythology for entertainment. This is about remembering the core energies that shape how you move through the world, your posture, your presence, your truth. Archetypes reveal what you stand for, even in silence.

You don't become embodied just by knowing your wounds. You become embodied by choosing how to channel your healed energy. Are you walking through life like the Victim, unconsciously waiting to be rescued? Or are you anchoring the grounded presence of the Healer, the wisdom of the Elder, the clarity of the Warrior, the devotion of the Mother, or the truth of the Visionary?

Each of us holds these energies within. The question is: which ones are active? Which ones are wounded? Which ones are asleep in your bones, waiting to be reawakened not through performance, but through lived truth?

This conversation is an invitation to recognise that your embodiment isn't just personal, it's archetypal. When you truly live in your frequency, you carry something far larger than your name or your narrative. You become a vessel for the collective. You become a mirror for others. You become a stabilizer in chaos, a lighthouse in fog. Not because you try to be but because you are anchored in energies older than culture and deeper than logic.

This is the art of archetypal embodiment. It builds upon everything we've explored so far: self-awareness, nervous system regulation, conscious boundaries, integrity, and aligned action. And now it moves us into the realm of **soulful leadership**, not the leadership of followers and applause, but the leadership of presence.

Let's walk into this with reverence, not as a checklist of traits, but as a return to deeper knowing. Because who you choose to embody... is the legacy you leave behind.

To embody an archetype is not to imitate a stereotype; it's to activate and live a deep principle of life from the inside out. You're not playing a role. You *are* becoming an instrument of that essence in your thoughts, posture, choices, reactions, and influence. These archetypes are not limited to professions or personal stories. They are energetic codes that express differently in each person's life, depending on what the moment calls for. Let's explore them not as frozen identities, but as dynamic living energies.

The Mother

The Mother is not just a parent or caretaker. She is the archetype of creation, nourishment, and holding. She brings life into form, whether it's a child, an idea, a community, or a vision. Her power lies in her capacity to *tend* to grow without control, to *nurture* without becoming the rescuer. She holds space for transformation, allowing others to evolve in her presence without imposing her will.

Embodied Mother energy is felt in those who can stay grounded while others process chaos. It is present in the teacher who encourages without smothering, the friend who listens without fixing, the leader who nurtures growth without making it about herself. The shadow side of the unintegrated Mother archetype is overgiving, martyrdom, or smothering, trying to control in the name of love. True Mother energy honors the autonomy of what she births.

The Warrior

The Warrior is the force of aligned action. Contrary to popular notions, this archetype is not about violence or domination. It is about standing in truth, setting boundaries, and acting with courage even when it's inconvenient. The Warrior does not fight from ego; he fights from soul. His discipline is born from devotion, not fear.

An embodied Warrior knows when to step forward and when to step back. He does not leak energy through performative anger or approval-seeking assertiveness. He walks into conflict with clarity, knowing what's worth protecting and what's just an illusion of threat. In daily life, this archetype shows up in how you honor your time, how you protect your peace, and how you say no, not from rejection, but from alignment.

The shadow Warrior is reactive, hypervigilant, or addicted to winning. The embodied Warrior is steady, intentional, and fights only for what matters.

The Healer

The Healer is not the fixer or savior. This archetype emerges from one who has faced their own wounds, walked through the fire, and learned to alchemize pain into wisdom. Embodied Healers are not attached to helping as an identity; they become a field of presence where healing naturally arises.

They don't impose methods. They don't rush someone's process. Their power lies in their stillness, their listening, their ability to hold paradox and witness pain without collapsing into it. They don't carry the burden of others; they have space for others to carry themselves.

In daily life, you embody the Healer when you allow others their path, when you stop enabling, and when you speak truth that liberates, even if it disrupts comfort. The shadow Healer tries to earn love by being needed. The mature Healer knows presence is more powerful than fixing.

The Leader

The Leader is not about control, charisma, or attention. It's about energetic responsibility. A real Leader doesn't push from ego; they *pull* through resonance. They don't dictate. They align. They know their frequency is contagious, so they tend to it with care. They influence not by dominating the room, but by being so rooted in integrity that others feel safe to rise.

Embodied leadership is not a performance. It's not about having followers. It's about being someone others trust because your actions, words, and presence are congruent. In small moments, the Leader chooses alignment over popularity. In big moments, the Leader doesn't collapse under pressure or inflate with praise.

The shadow of the Leader archetype is superiority, savior complex, or control disguised as service. The embodied Leader knows their role is to hold the field, not to be the hero of the story.

The Sovereign

While not consistently named, the Sovereign is the archetype that anchors the others. It's the one who owns their life fully, not through dominance, but through self-responsibility. The Sovereign doesn't wait for permission. They know who they are, and they know that their inner world shapes their outer reality.

This archetype is expressed in how you make decisions, how you handle failure, and how you honor your values without needing external validation. The Sovereign is not about ruling others, it's about ruling your inner world with grace, discipline, and clarity.

Archetypes as Embodied Intelligence

These aren't characters to switch in and out of. In truth, you carry all of them. At different times, one may lead while another retreats to the background. You may find yourself in Warrior mode during conflict, in Healer mode during a friend's breakdown, in Leader mode when holding space for a group, and in Mother mode when nurturing your own healing.

The point is not to perfect one or the other but to allow their mature essence to live through you, moment to moment. Not just as ideas. But as instincts. Movements. Boundaries. Tone. Silence. The way you listen. The way you rise. The way you stay.

True embodiment means these archetypes don't stay locked in books or mythology. They walk with you. Through you. And as you embody them with integrity, the world around you starts to shift not through force, but through frequency.

Once we recognize these archetypes as internal blueprints rather than distant ideals, we begin to notice their presence in our lives and how they inspire us to live more fully. The process of embodiment focuses on integration, a significant act of allowing these energies to influence your life through awareness and conscious practice.

In Relationships:

In our romantic, familial, and social interactions, our archetypes provide opportunities for growth and connection. The Wounded Child encourages us to seek comfort and support, while embodying the Lover brings presence, curiosity, and deep attention, creating a space of safety and intimacy.

Mother energy shines through nurturing without entanglement, offering grounded care without the urge to fix. The Warrior expresses clear boundaries that honor truth, allowing you to affirm, "I love you, and I still honor myself." The Healer listens deeply, helping others hear themselves while embodying a steadfast presence with no agenda, no ego, just attuned awareness. In authentic relationships, embodying these archetypes manifests not in grand gestures but in the tone of your voice, the steadiness of your gaze, the choice to pause before reacting, and the ability to withstand discomfort with grace.

In Work And Creativity:

Your work integrates seamlessly with your archetypes. The Leader archetype embodies energetic integrity, standing firm amidst chaos and leading from your inner vision. The Creator channels divine intelligence into tangible forms, diving in, playing, molding, and iterating. This energy encompasses expression rather than perfection. The Magician identifies patterns others may overlook, bridging the gap between logic and intuition, structure and spirit. When you create something that feels channeled or birth a project that seems "bigger than you," you are embodying the Magician.

Engaging in embodied work aligns your productivity with your body's natural rhythm, intertwining your vision with service and avoiding hustle in favour of transmission.

In Parenting Or Mentoring:

Embodying archetypes in parenting arises from being grounded in the qualities you wish to pass on. The Mother archetype imparts emotional attunement through safety and presence, fostering an environment where children can thrive. The Elder archetype guides with humility, embodying presence in mentorship or parenting. The Protector scans the environment with care, establishing sacred structures that support growth.

Embodied parenting emphasizes safety, clarity, and grace, communicating values far beyond words.

In Leadership:

The most effective leaders anchor a room rather than dominate it. They embody the Leader archetype as a commitment to coherence, listening more than they speak and transmuting chaos. Real leadership draws from the Warrior, safeguarding what is sacred and upholding values with courage. It also emerges from the Healer, who understands the need for systemic healing and embodies the change they wish to create. The Visionary dares to envision a better world, aligning with that vision even when others cannot see it yet.

An embodied leader magnetizes through energetic integrity, inspiring trust before speaking because of their inner work.

In Daily Life:

In everyday routines, these archetypes reveal themselves in subtle yet meaningful ways: in how you enjoy your morning tea, respond to a stranger's gaze, handle uncertainty, nourish your body, and honor your time. The Priestess or Devotee emerges when you sweep the floor as if it were sacred ground. The Sovereign arises when you enter a room feeling at home in yourself, taking up space with assurance.

CHAPTER 16: THE ART OF LIVING IT

Embodiment is not a theory, it is a practice. The difference between knowing and living is where transformation happens. Many of us can speak the language of awareness, we can describe conditioning, name wounds, and quote wisdom, but until those truths touch our everyday choices, they remain abstract. The art of living it is where ideas step off the page and enter your body, your home, your relationships, and your presence.

From Insight To Integration

Think of the moment after reading a powerful book or

hearing a moving talk. For a few hours, even days, you feel inspired, almost glowing. But then life rushes back in: emails, family obligations, old triggers. The insight is still true, but it fades into the background because it hasn't been integrated. Living it means building bridges between insight and action.

For example, imagine you've realized that silence at the dinner table is not always peace but often suppression. Awareness alone might make you angry at your family, or sad about your past. But the art of living it would be trying something small: gently sharing one honest sentence during the next conversation, even if your voice shakes. That is embodiment. Not waiting for perfect conditions, but practicing truth in the spaces that once silenced you.

The Daily Rituals Of Alignment

Living in alignment doesn't require radical life changes overnight. It asks for small, consistent choices that reflect your inner truth.

- When your body asks for rest, you honor it with a pause rather than another cup of coffee.
- When your heart signals "no," you speak it, even if it disappoints someone.
- When you feel joy, you let it be seen without apology.

Each of these is simple, but together they build a life that feels whole.

I remember a woman from one of my workshops who always said yes to family demands. She thought love meant constant sacrifice. After we worked on boundaries, she decided to try something radical — saying "I'll think about it" instead of instantly agreeing. At first, it felt terrifying. But slowly, she discovered that her family respected her more when she honored her own time. That single shift rippled into her work, her friendships, and even her health. This is what it means to live it: not to escape life, but to transform it from within.

The Courage To Be Ordinary

One of the greatest misconceptions about alignment is that it must look extraordinary, retreats in Bali, perfect routines, flawless mornings. In reality, the art of living it is often quiet and ordinary. It is how you breathe when you wake up, how you greet the stranger in the market, how you treat yourself when you forget something important.

Take the example of Arjun, who once believed his worth came only from his corporate performance. When he left that job, he struggled with shame: Who am I if I'm not producing? Slowly, he began practicing presence in ordinary acts. Making his morning tea without rushing. Walking to the park without headphones. Calling a friend without an agenda. These were not glamorous acts, but they were radical, because they rewired his nervous system to feel safe in simply being.

Living In Relationship

Embodiment is tested most not in solitude but in relationship. It is easy to feel spiritual while meditating alone; the challenge comes when your partner criticizes you or your parent repeats an old script.

Living it means noticing your trigger and choosing a new response. Instead of shutting down, you might breathe and say, "I need a moment before I respond." Instead of people-pleasing, you might allow silence to hold the weight of your truth.

Relationships become the dojo of embodiment, the place where the practices are sharpened, where old patterns reappear and where new choices take root.

Returning To The Body

The art of living it is also literal: it is lived in the body. Our bodies carry the imprints of wounds and conditioning, but they also carry the key to presence. To live aligned, you must listen.

Ask yourself:

- Where in my body do I feel truth?
- Where do I feel the tension of self-betrayal?
- What happens in my chest, stomach, or throat when I silence myself?

For example, one reader once told me that every time she lied, even small white lies, she felt a burning in her throat. It wasn't random. Her body was signaling the dissonance between words and truth. As she began to honor that signal, her voice grew stronger. She stopped saying "I'm fine" when she wasn't. That simple shift began a cascade of change: her relationships grew more authentic, her energy returned, and her sense of self deepened.

Legacy In Motion

Ultimately, the art of living it is not about perfection but about practice. Each choice is a brushstroke in the painting of your life. Some strokes will be messy, some bold, some hesitant. But together, they create a masterpiece of integrity.

When you embody alignment, you don't just change yourself. You shift the frequency of every room you enter. Your children watch, your friends notice, strangers feel it. Living it becomes your legacy, not through titles or achievements, but through the energy you leave behind.

And this is the invitation: not to collect wisdom, but to embody it. Not to perform a role, but to live your truth in the small and the vast, the ordinary and the sacred. Because the art of living it is nothing less than the art of being fully alive.

AFTERWORD

There is no final lesson. There is only living it.

No matter how many books you read or insights you gather, the true shift will always happen in your body, your relationships, your moment-to-moment awareness.

There will be days when your alignment feels effortless, and others when you return to old survival patterns. That's okay. The path of embodiment is not about being perfect, it's about being honest.

Let this be your invitation to keep coming back. To pause. To listen. To move from the inner "yes" rather than the external noise.

You are not here to perform a better self. You are here to *become more fully you* again and again, with compassion, integrity, and presence.

And if you ever forget: come back to your breath. Come back to your body. Come back to your truth.

NOTES

This book is a reflection of lived experience, deep inquiry, and collected wisdom across traditions of psychology, spirituality, and healing. It is not a replacement for therapy, medical treatment, or professional support. Please use discernment and seek guidance when necessary.

REFERENCES

The ideas in this book have been shaped by both personal exploration and the work of thinkers, writers, and researchers across time:

- Carl Jung — *Collected Works*
- Alice Miller — *The Drama of the Gifted Child*
- Gabor Maté — *When the Body Says No*
- Bessel van der Kolk — *The Body Keeps the Score*
- Research from the Adverse Childhood Experiences (ACE) Study
- Epigenetic studies on intergenerational trauma

FURTHER READING & LISTENING

For those wishing to go deeper, here are books and podcasts that resonate with the themes of creativity, healing, and alignment:

Books

- Julia Cameron — *The Artist's Way*
- Elizabeth Gilbert — *Big Magic: Creative Living Beyond Fear*
- Clarissa Pinkola Estés — *Women Who Run With the Wolves*
- Eckhart Tolle — *The Power of Now*
- Pema Chödrön — *When Things Fall Apart*
- Tara Brach — *Radical Acceptance*
- Mark Wolynn — *It Didn't Start With You*

- Michael Singer — *The Untethered Soul*
- Don Miguel Ruiz — *The Four Agreements*

Podcasts

- *The Tim Ferriss Show* (exploring creativity, performance, and inner growth)
- *The Mel Robbins Podcast* (practical mindset shifts and empowerment)
- *On Being with Krista Tippett* (conversations on meaning, faith, and humanity)
- *Unlocking Us* by Brené Brown (courage, vulnerability, and leadership)
- *Awaken and Align* by Deepshikha (your own podcast, aligning personal stories with universal truths)

www.ingramcontent.com/pod-product-compliance
Ingram Content Group UK Ltd.
Pitfield, Milton Keynes, MK11 3LW, UK
UKHW021402190726
13845UKWH00028B/822

9 788198 000194